THE MEDICI

HARPER TORCHBOOKS / The Cloister Library

(Continued on next page)

HARPER TORCHBOOKS / The Academy Library

HARPER TORCHBOOKS / The Science Library

FERDINAND SCHEVILL

THE MEDICI

HARPER TORCHBOOKS / *The Academy Library*

HARPER & BROTHERS · PUBLISHERS · NEW YORK

To the Casa de Marita
and its Inspired Designer

CONTENTS

vii

Contents

ILLUSTRATIONS

Following page 66

ix

INTRODUCTORY

IT IS not surprising that the usurpation of the republic of Florence by the family of the Medici should have been the occasion of a lively political controversy. It is much more surprising that the controversy should have been sustained through the subsequent centuries down to our own day. One group of writers, generally speaking native Florentines, have regarded the Medici and their rule with outspoken aversion; another group, natives in the main of the countries lying beyond the Alps, have condoned their seizure of power and taken a favorable view of their conduct of office. Some members of this latter group, not content with lauding their political rule, have lavished especial praise on their services to culture. Although such unqualified encomiasts belong largely to a past period, their attitude has not been entirely abandoned and may still be encountered in works of recent date.[1]

The present writer is of the opinion that a work on the Medici which, avoiding both enmity and partisanship, follows a middle course, may render a useful service to the perhaps dwindling but still sizable body of readers who resort to history for

[1] As an example of a presentation of this uncritically laudatory character enjoying a wide popularity we may mention the work entitled *The Medici* by Col. G. F. Young.

the double purpose of cultural enrichment and such light on the unfathomed nature of man as his story, wherever sampled, may yield. His proposed work will carry the main tested facts pertaining to both the political and the cultural activities of the Medici and offer an appraisal of the successive heads of the house in their double role. However, since Cosimo, founder of the family's fortunes did not gain the mastery of Florence until the relatively late year in its history of 1434, it will be necessary to review, though with blurring brevity, the earlier story of the Arno city. Unless this is done, Cosimo's appearance on the scene will find us in the dark regarding the situation which he faced and the line of action he adopted. It will at once appear that no sooner had he appropriated the political power than he assumed also the part of patron of literature and art. It admits of no doubt that this action comported with his character. And yet it may also be said that it was fairly forced on him by the powerful traditions of the society of which he had become the official head.

The Florentine society of Cosimo's day owed the extraordinary empire it wielded over its members to its brilliant achievements of the preceding two to three hundred years. Many of these achievements belong to the socio-political sphere and embrace signal improvements in government and definitely startling innovations in trade and industry. Their combined operation explains the eminence among the cities of the world attained by Florence long before the name of the Medici was ever bruited in its busy streets and squares. If we now add the accumulation during these same pre-Medicean centuries of a body of intellectual and artistic achievements which shone even farther afield than the impressive material triumphs, it will become clear and indisputable that the first step toward the proper understanding of the Medici is to accept them as latecomers in a long-established, highly developed society moving forward under its own unexhausted energies. These energies, as had been the case from the beginning, still flowed from their original well-spring, the Florentine people, and justified the boast that the people were the fashioners of both the novel institutions and the spiritual culture passing under their name. In the light of this blunt and irrefutable statement, the view, still not infrequently aired, that the Florentine greatness and, particularly, its cultural greatness stem from the ruling family is completely lacking in foundation. What the Medici did, and what in the nature of the case was all they could do, was to make a contribution to that greatness in their time. To set this forth as fully as space permits will be an important concern of this book. Its leading concern, however, will be to examine the Medici for their own sake and to follow with concentrated attention their conduct of the public affairs of one of the most intelligent and fascinating communities carried in the annals of history.

From the continuing controversies touching the Medici here lightly indicated, it follows that the successive phases through which Florentine society passed in the centuries before the advent of Cosimo must needs be set forth as the indispensable curtain-raiser to our main matter.

I

ORIGIN AND GROWTH OF THE COMMUNE OF FLORENCE: FROM DEPENDENCE TO INDEPENDENCE

IN SHARP distinction from Fiesole, an ancient hill-town of remote Etruscan origin, Florence, in the valley of the Arno below Fiesole, was founded as a Roman colony under a law promulgated in 59 B.C. during the consulship of Julius Caesar. It was laid out on a modest scale in the form of the square commonly adopted by the Roman army on making camp and was surrounded by a wall, the line of which can still be traced within the vastly expanded city of the present day. Roman Florence never rose above the importance of a small provincial center. The Roman ruins, located by modern archaeological research many feet below the existing street levels, give evidence that the town must have been a miniature reproduction of the imperial capital. It declined in sympathetic response to the decline of the empire of which it was a part, and in the course of the devastating barbarian invasions shriveled to a hollow shell. Of its existence in the succeeding age of darkness, which constitutes the earliest phase of what is commonly called the Middle Ages, only a few stray facts have come down to us. While they give evidence that the town had not perished, they disclose that no more than the barest life pulsed through its sparsely populated streets.

From their long winter sleep Florence and the other Italian towns were slow to arouse themselves and put an end to the succession of blighted centuries which intervene between the passing of the Greco-Roman and the rise of the new Western civilization. The most striking consequence of the destructive Germanic invasions had been the replacement of the Roman cities and their urban culture with the purely agrarian system carrying the name of feudalism. Reduced to its simplest expression, feudalism was a system of land tenure under which a relatively small body of armed landowners lived by the labor of disarmed peasants held in varying degrees of serfdom. Under feudalism, which constituted a social order hardly a shade above anarchy, the once excellent Roman roads fell into decay, safe and peaceful travel practically ceased, and trade took on the primitive form of barter and became limited in the main to communities within easy hail of one another. While commerce of a wider range in such articles of pressing need as salt and iron never quite died out, it was conducted on a small scale and attended by innumerable risks due to the absence of an effective central government and to the universal insecurity of life and property.

Around the year A.D. 1000 came a change. It was inaugurated by an increased measure of public security accompanied by a gradual intensification of the overland movement of goods. Their oversea movement continued to lag because the Mohammedan powers had brought the great central water, the Mediterranean Sea, under their unchallenged control. Not until the age of the crusades was their monopoly broken with the result that the Italian cities, as closest to the reopened communication lanes, became the earliest beneficiaries of the renewed exchange between east and west. Awakening trade revived the drowsy towns, which in their turn brought the industrial crafts again to life, drew the peasant-serfs into the towns in the hope of improving their condition, and led to the birth of a vigorous civic pride. This manifested itself in the gradual creation of novel municipal functions and in a gathering spirit of resistance to the feudal oppressors of the countryside.

While the urban revival first made its appearance in the rich plains of Lombardy, it was quick to leap the Appenines and take possession of Tuscany, where, in every town, it produced a substantially identical transformation. The emerging class of adventuring merchants formed protective associations called guilds, the craftsmen followed the example of the bolder merchant element by forming craft guilds, and under the general revival of enterprise the extremely rudimentary town government expanded its activities by taking over such common concerns as the supply of water, the enforcement of order by police and courts, and an organized resistance to the feudal landowners who roamed the highways and plundered the merchant caravans.

The indicated developments covered many generations and took place in so gradual and concealed a manner that there is not a single town of either Lombardy or Tuscany for which they can any longer be recovered in satisfactory detail. For Florence, more particularly, there is a distressing scarcity of evidence which it is permissible cautiously to supplement by drawing on the parallel and frequently better documented development of its Tuscan neighbors. Thus, although the earliest mention in a surviving record of a Florentine merchant guild belongs to the year 1182, its birth may confidently be asserted to lie further back. Supporting evidence derives from Pisa which, as a coastal city, revived before inland Florence and for which a merchant guild can be proved at a much earlier date. By the same kind of deduction there were craft guilds in Florence before 1193, which is the earliest year of their mention in an existing record.

Similar reasoning in connection with the political developments that invariably accompanied the economic ones yields similar fruit. Whenever a reawakened town felt the need of providing for a new civic interest that had come into existence with the economic revival, the situation was met by the appointment of an executive committee of trustworthy citizens. Called *boni homines,* they attended to the particular business with which they were charged and, after reporting on it to a special council or perhaps even to the general assembly of the townsmen, were honorably dismissed. In the course of time these purely temporary committees were replaced by a committee of a more permanent character expressive of the improved municipal consolidation. When that stage was reached the original committee name of boni homines was dropped in favor of the more resounding name of consuls. Without doubt the new designation owed its adoption to the swelling sense of power which moved the town dwellers to assimilate their new creation to the long-vanished but unforgotten Roman republic.

The appearance of consuls in any Italian commune may be accepted as evidence that it has reached a relatively advanced stage of municipal organization. It also indicated that the commune was engaged in detaching itself from the dominant feudal system in which it was imbedded in order to become free and independent. The first authoritative reference to consuls in the case of Florence belongs to the year 1138. But since for other Tuscan communes, and especially for the older Pisa, the coastal leader in the communal movement, they can be proved for a much earlier date, we are on safe ground when we assert that the stage of development signified by this name had already been reached by Florence by the turn of the century.

The form assumed by the Florentine municipal constitution in the period of the consuls, that is, summarily viewed, in the twelfth century, varies only in unimportant details from its form throughout the Italian town area and presents the following leading features. The consuls were a plural executive, usually of twelve men, whose term of office ran for a year. Their functions were described in a document called *breve consulum,* which served as a constitution and on which the incoming consuls took their oath of office. The general assembly of the citizens was called *parlamentum* and, in theory at least, was regarded as the ultimate source of political power. In practice, however, it yielded place to a *concilium* or council of about one hundred and fifty members drawn from the upper stratum of the population. This top-level group was composed of landowners who, though residents of the town, were endowed with manors (or farmsteads) in the immediate neighborhood and of merchants who had accumulated wealth by trade. By frequent intermarriage landowners and merchants were fused into a single class of the well-to-do and so decidedly exercised control that the consuls invariably issued from their number. If the existence of the parlamentum lent the consular system a certain appearance of democracy, it is indisputable that in practice it operated as a narrow oligarchy.

Since the self-governing municipality of Florence was a revolutionary creation planted in the midst of a hostile feudal world, it was obliged from the first moment of its existence to fight for its life. The countryside round about was in the hands of small nobles, who owed allegiance to greater nobles, who, in their turn, owed allegiance to the emperor. Had the members of this hierarchically ordered caste held together in accordance with their oath of fealty, they might have hindered or at least have seriously delayed the triumph of the communes. But they cantankerously quarreled and fought with each other and were besides in frequent revolt against their supreme head. As for this apex of the system, it greatly weakened his authority that he was a foreigner from across the Alps and usually so occupied with the affairs of Germany, where his main power lay, that he was obliged to absent himself for extended periods from his

Italian dependency. The result was that the new and, let us always remember, revolutionary town governments were enabled to take by assault the castles of the noblemen of their immediate neighborhood and reduce their owners to subjection. Whenever on the heels of a development of this nature a German king and emperor appeared in Italy, the outraged nobles would crowd about him, clamoring for redress against the presumptuous communes. Overawed by the sovereign's might, these revolutionary bodies would then sulkily annul their illegal appropriations. However, no sooner had the emperor turned homeward and again put the Alps between himself and Italy than they would resume their aggressions and re-assert the control of the countryside, which was absolutely indispensable to their continued existence.

At last—it was the year 1154—an emperor came to Italy resolved to put an end to this trifling with the majesty of the law and his own inherited dignity. He was Frederick of the house of Hohenstaufen, to whom the Italians, struck by his flaming beard, gave the name of Barbarossa. On descending the Alps, he set foot in Lombardy and gave his outraged attention to the communal audacities by which his and his vassals' power had been effectively destroyed. The scene before his eyes showed that many more than a score of towns had once again given themselves unauthorized republican governments and had once again laid their yoke on the nobles of their immediate neighborhood. By sweepingly declaring these developments null and void, the redbeard emperor issued a challenge, which, on their recovering from their first confusion, the communes met by united resistance. For many agitated years the decision between the contestants, representative respectively of the dead hand of the law and the right inherent in social change, hung fire until at last, in 1176, the towns won the overwhelming victory of Legnano. The humbled sovereign was forced to accept a settlement, the terms of which were drawn up seven years later, in 1183, at the city of Constance in Germany. By this treaty the members of the Lombard League of cities won all the essential rights, on the free exercise of which they had staked life and goods.

In the rights won by the Lombard communes at Constance, their Tuscan sisters, who had kept aloof from the grueling struggle in Lombardy, acquired no share. However, having, like their Lombard neighbors, illegally seized these rights before the coming of Barbarossa to Italy, they clung to them as long as the situation permitted. It followed that whenever the emperor's power exceeded their own, which, owing to the long seesaw of the Lombard conflict, was often the case, they made or at least feigned submission to their liege. It was a fatal source of weakness that since they never sufficiently overcame their bitter rivalries to form a league among themselves after the Lombard model, they faced the emperor separately and alone and, thus divided, were inescapably at his mercy. Before his reign came to a close with his death on crusade in the year 1190, he had succeeded not only in sustaining but in actually strengthening the feudal regime in Tuscany by means of a novel central administration, which, without exactly destroying the self-government of the towns, reduced it to very slender proportions.

In this humbled condition the Tuscan communes remained throughout the reign of Frederick's son and successor. This was Henry VI, who, a man hard as flint and of unusual ability, kept the administrative machinery fashioned by his father in effective operation. However, the moment the news of his death in southern Italy, which occurred in 1197, reached Tuscany, the towns at last and with amazing unanimity formed the league, which, owing to their mutual rancor, they had thus far been unable to achieve. Thus fortified, they not only promptly resumed their former self-government but, in addition, each town asserted sovereignty over its *contado* or county and with the least possible delay brought every castle-owner within the county's compass into subjection to its rule. The revolutionary action was greatly favored by the circumstance that Henry VI's heir was a three-year-old boy and that, since the German crown was elective and not hereditary, the German princes were unwilling to raise a child to the throne. To deepen the confusion a disputed election took place in Germany which completely paralyzed the imperial power and left the Tuscan towns in undisputed mastery of the situation. Not till 1215 were the disabling conditions beyond the Alps remedied by the election to the German throne of Henry VI's son and heir, now arrived at man's estate. Named after his grandfather, he became Emperor Frederick II and with a born fighter's energy and a born politician's lack of scruple undertook to revive the shattered imperial authority by again reducing the rebellious communes of both Tuscany and Lombardy to imperial subjection.

The long reign of the exceptionally gifted Frederick II (1215-1250) constitutes the final stage in the long conflict between the inherited feudal system whose summit was the emperor and the revolutionary system of communal self-government represented by the towns. It is marked by many breathless crises for which there is no room in this abbreviated tale. Suffice it that the battle raged up and down the peninsula and that Frederick might have achieved at least a temporary victory had it not been for the intervention of the pope.

The head of the church thus brought belatedly into our account of the conflict that had been rocking Italy for well over a century had in point of fact been a major figure in it from the start. This was not because there was anything in the nature of the papacy which from internal necessity moved its representative to align himself with the communes. On the contrary, the pope was as closely integrated with the feudal system as the emperor himself and was far from feeling any instinctive sympathy with the democratic aspirations of the towns. However, he had a quarrel of his own with the emperor which considerably antedated the latter's quarrel with the communes. By universally accepted medieval theory pope and emperor were the two closely co-ordinated heads of Christendom, each supreme in his particular sphere. This for the emperor was the realm of civil government, for the pope the realm of spiritual government institutionally identified with the church. The theory was predicated on the smooth interaction of church and state to the end of giving effect to the assumed plan of a benign Creator for the salvation of the sinful progeny of Adam. In practice, however, it proved impossible to draw a clean and incontestable dividing line between the two supposedly harmonious powers. As a result their respective representatives were engaged in an all but uninterrupted struggle with each other over their respective areas of authority throughout the protracted medieval centuries.

As against the emperor's formidable physical power the pope in general depended in his struggle with his rival on nothing more ponderable than moral power. Surprisingly, in modern eyes, it so fully sufficed that he issued victorious from every major conflict with his opponent. Before ever the freedom of the towns had become a fighting issue he had scored a triumph so impressive that it has become indelibly imprinted on the memory of men. In the bitter month of January, 1077, the young Emperor Henry IV, whom Pope Gregory VII had excommunicated, that is, had formally ejected from the Christian community, stood for three days in the snow and ice of the castle yard of Canossa in the Apennines humbly pleading for admission to the papal presence that he might learn what penance he must do before he would be readmitted to the Christian fold. Then, exactly one hundred years later, in 1177, the atrium of the ancient church of San Marco at Venice witnessed a similar papal triumph. The penitent emperor on the later occasion was the famous Barbarossa, who had just been catastrophically defeated by the Lombard communes closely allied with Pope Alexander III. During an early phase of the conflict, when Frederick seemed on the point of forcing the towns to their knees, without any even remote prompting of affection for the democratically oriented communes Alexander had unhesitatingly thrown in his lot with them for no other reason than his fear of the consequences for himself of the threatened imperial victory. So decisive did his influence on the minds of men, his purely moral influence, prove that he was a leading factor in the final victory of the towns. Consequently, on suing for an accommodation, Frederick was obliged, as a condition preliminary to peace with the League of Lombard cities, to make submission to the triumphant pope. Hence the dramatic scene at San Marco. Prostrating himself before the enthroned Alexander to kiss his foot, the defeated emperor furnished renewed evidence that a struggle between the two putative heads of Christendom was certain to end in a papal victory.

Returning to the resumption by the grandson of Barbarossa of the attempt to reduce the Italian towns to submission, we will readily agree that the papal contemporaries of Frederick II must have been as fearful as their predecessors had been of the consequences for the papal office of the emperor's victory. It will therefore cause no surprise that first, Pope Gregory IX (1227-1241) and, after him, Pope Innocent IV (1243-1254) took their stand at the side of the towns. By so doing they succeeded in establishing what for many years resulted in a substantial balance of forces. Then, with the fiercely contested struggle between emperor and communes still undecided, fate took a hand in the game by the removal of Frederick from the scene by his death on December 3, 1250. As at the touch of a magician's wand the Italian situation assumed an entirely different aspect. Frederick's young son and successor was so hampered by rebellion in Germany that he could not promptly cross the Alps; and when he did come he died before he had developed sufficient power to make his presence felt. Not only, in consequence, did the unmolested towns recover their liberties but a far-seen milestone of Italian history was set up by the empire's passing into such deep eclipse that the peninsula was henceforth free to employ its released and unbounded energies for its own ends without interference by a foreign master.

A development that had attended the last phase of the struggle between empire and towns demands consideration at this point.

The long-drawn-out conflict had sharply divided opinion and produced throughout the peninsula a conservative party backing Frederick and his feudal supporters and an opposition party fervidly enlisted for the republican system of the communes and their papal ally. Inevitably each party took on an appropriate· appellation, the partisans of the empire calling themselves Ghibellines and their opponents taking the name of Guelphs.[1] Although it cannot be doubted that the independence of the towns was the leading subject of contention between the two parties, the fact that the pope was accepted by the Guelphs as their titular head lent a certain plausibility to the notion that the Guelphs were primarily a church party. However, while it is, generally speaking, true that the Guelphs gave the pope their firm devotion, it is no less true that they did so in overwhelming measure because they needed his strength to buttress the republican cause. Even before the death of Frederick II and under the influence of the political division occasioned by his policy, the Ghibellines of Tuscany, Lombardy, and every other province of Italy had begun to stand together in a loosely organized provincial party; and the Guelphs followed the same pattern. Consequently, although no successor to Frederick II appeared in Italy for the next fifty years, the Guelph-Ghibelline conflict continued to constitute the core and substance of Italian history because, although communal freedom was now no longer in imminent peril, its enemy, feudalism, had not been destroyed and lustily continued the struggle.

This very summary picture of the general Italian situation during the thirteenth century is offered to no other purpose than to supply the peninsular framework for the local Florentine developments, which are our main concern. On last considering our town on the middle Arno we noted that it had be-

[1] These party names derived from Germany, where the reigning house of Hohenstaufen was opposed by the house of Welf. The latter name accommodated to the Italian tongue became Guelph. Ghibelline is more of a problem, since it represents the more violent distortion of the word Waiblingen. This name, a castle of the Hohenstaufen family, was imported into Italy by making itself heard as the battle cry shouted by the charging army of the emperor.

come a self-governing commune under a regime of elected consuls. Since, as we noted at the same time, the consuls were regularly chosen from an upper, well-to-do citizen stratum, it came about that bitter jealousies and family feuds developed which frequently led to prolonged and bloody brawling in the narrow streets. With such excesses periodically paralyzing the government recourse was had to a cure already tried out by similarly afflicted neighbors. It consisted in calling to the headship of the commune for the term of a year a capable foreigner unaffected by the family rivalries which so seriously embarrassed the unhappy consular government. He was given the title *podestà* and without question succeeded in instituting an improved social order. It was around the year 1200 that Florence, and most other Italian towns as well, abandoned the multiple consular executive in favor of the single foreign podestà. While he would appear to have mitigated the grave municipal disturbances, he cannot, as an appointive official endowed with special judicial powers, by any stretch of the imagination be held to mark an advance in democratic organization.

Throughout the stormy years of Emperor Frederick II's frenzied attempt to turn back the clock the necessary but undemocratic podestà continued to figure as the leading official of Florence. Then, on Frederick's death in 1250, with a revolutionary energy that would not be denied, the pent-up democratic waters burst the dykes. Sweeping the hitherto all-powerful upper citizen class aside, the people set up the first and, in a certain sense, the only truly democratic regime the town ever had. In witness of its popular character it has been designated in Florentine annals as *il primo populo* or the First Democracy. Brought into being by an anti-imperial explosion, it was of course a Guelph regime and promptly aspired to make all Tuscany Guelph and bring it under Florentine control. This was a program which maddened the Ghibellines and led to a savage resistance to Florence and the Guelphs centered in the two traditionally Ghibelline towns of Siena and Pisa. Startlingly impotent against the energetic Florentine aggression, the Ghibellines were held in complete check until they received support from the revival of the Hohenstaufen cause in Frederick II's hereditary dominion, the kingdom of Sicily. Here his illegitimate son, Manfred, had gained possession of the throne and recklessly threw his weight into the Tuscan scales against Guelph Florence.

The result was that after a brilliant ten-year ascendancy the First Democracy came to a catastrophic close when, in 1260, at Montaperti under the walls of neighboring Siena, the Sienese army, led by the cavalry contingent sent by King Manfred, crushingly defeated the Florentine host with its numerous Guelph allies. Pursuing the fleeing enemy to the gates of Florence, the Ghibellines entered the undefended city, banished such leading Guelphs as had not already sought safety in flight, and took over the government. By following through with the same policy in the other towns of the province they converted all Tuscany into a united Ghibelline stronghold.

This was a development so offensive to Pope Clement IV that he was prepared to adopt extreme measures to end its intolerable humiliation. Excommunicating and deposing King Manfred, he offered the crown of Sicily to Charles of Anjou, brother of the French king, Louis IX, and promised to support the invader with all the financial resources of the church. The struggle that followed is crowded with some of the most dramatic incidents within the whole range of medieval history. We must regretfully content ourselves with the unadorned facts. Duly crowned king of Sicily by the pope in 1265, Charles of Anjou marched against Manfred and in February, 1266, at Beneventum, overwhelmed him so utterly that when the day ended Manfred lay, a disfigured corpse, upon the battlefield. The resurgent Guelphs were jubilant but their victory was not yet complete. In 1268 the last male member of the Hohenstaufen line, a sixteen-year-old lad named Conradin, crossed the Alps with the double intent of buttressing the shaken Ghibelline cause and of recovering his lost Sicilian kingdom. In August of that year, at Tagliacozzo, he was, like his uncle, Manfred, before him, defeated by the usurper, Charles, and, while he did not perish on the battlefield, suffered a much grimmer fate by being carried a prisoner to Naples, where he was beheaded as a common felon in the market-place of that sunbathed southern city.

With this victory the Ghibelline overthrow was complete and the Guelphs, triumphant through the military might of King Charles, had become the undisputed masters of Tuscany. Florence, once more Guelph, not only exiled the Ghibellines in its midst but also, for good measure, ruined them beyond the chance of recovery by confiscating and distributing their property. However, the vanished regime of the First Democracy was not again set up. Final authority now rested with the Guelph party which, directed by the triumphant king of Sicily, favored a more aristocratic system. But the politically reactionary rule the king imposed did not hinder its representatives from stepping up contemporary merchant enterprise for the already noted reason that in Florence the nobles (or persons who rated as such) were by reason of their own past practices and by continued intermarriage with the leading merchant families hardly, if at all, distinguishable from the prosperous traders.

Consequently, it should not cause surprise that the Guelph pacification of Tuscany was attended by a Florentine economic boom that provided a greatly broadened base to the city's claim to provincial primacy. Its trade expanded so rapidly that it reached across the Alps as far as the flourishing towns of Flanders and northern France. The leading article of this far-ranging enterprise was the coarse woolen cloth, which, on being imported from northern Europe, was refined by special, locally developed techniques and re-exported to be sold at a higher price. Then, as their next step, the merchants undertook to supplement this trade by importing the wool itself and settled for this purpose on the excellent, long-stapled wool of England and Spain. By this widened activity they created a supplementary woolen in-

dustry which saw the cloth through every one of its many production stages. In a surprisingly short time the alert Florentine
industrialists achieved an undisputed leadership over their rivals,
Italian and foreign alike, and turned out what was generally
conceded to be the premier cloth of Europe. The many technical
and administrative manipulations required for its production at
home and its distribution abroad were concentrated in the hands
of merchant companies, which to give their far-flung activities
a sound financial basis, assumed also the functions of a bank.

The striking success of the merchant companies was greatly
promoted by the fact that under the First Democracy the government had had the foresight to issue a coin of its own, the
celebrated *fiorino d'oro,* or gold florin. Wisely minted at an un-
fluctuating gold content, it gained universal confidence and,
gradually replacing the many unreliable coins in general circulation, became the common monetary measure throughout the
western world. It may be left to the imagination how much the
spread of the habit of quoting prices in the native currency
boosted the Florentine prestige. The annual turnover of the
merchant companies steadily increased. Increased volume was
attended by increased wealth, which, far from being limited to
the merchants themselves, spread in a diminishing trickle to the
lower levels of the rapidly growing population. A further closely
related consequence was a considerably altered structure of society and this, according to a universally operative law, led to
a movement to bring the backward political government into
better accord with the socio-economic realities.

All this foreshadowed a new democratic movement, by which
when it arrived in 1282 the nobiliary government resting on the
might of King Charles was quietly superseded. The decisive step
was taken by the seven leading guilds, whose members constituted the business elite of the town. To ensure the success of
their seizure of power they took the precautionary measure of
associating with themselves in a subordinate capacity the five
leading craft guilds. As the Italian word for guild is *arte* and

as the merchant guilds were called the *arti maggiori* or major arts, it was substantially the major arts which in 1282 took over the government. Their precise action was to set up a new executive from their own membership called priors. The foreign podestà was not abolished but his functions were reduced and he was subordinated to the new magistracy. Six in number (later eight), the priors served for two months and, during their incumbency lived together as a single family in a private house hired for the purpose. Not till a generation later were they installed in their splendid new residence, the *Palazzo dei Signori,* now called the *Palazzo Vecchio* and still the most impressive reminder to native-born and foreigner alike of the medieval greatness of the city.

For the next ten years the new government of the priors led a rather precarious existence, owing to the opposition it encountered from the nobiliary elements which it had pushed aside. In their rancor they multiplied the excesses in which it was their custom to indulge against their humbler fellow citizens encountered in street and square. Owing to the inherited submissiveness of the common people and also because of the close family bonds existing between the merchant guildsmen and the high-stepping nobles effective measures to curb the upper class arrogance were for a time adjourned. Then, after a decade of increasingly impatient waiting, the priors at last summoned the courage to bring the issue to a head. They might not even then have acted, had not their hands been upheld by an inspired leader, Giano della Bella. As has not infrequently been the case in radical social transformations, the anti-noble, Giano, belonged by birth to the very class, the curbing of which had become a no longer adjournable civic necessity.

In January, 1293, the government of the priors under the powerful drive of Giano della Bella promulgated the most famous act of Florentine constitutional history, the Ordinances of Justice. It falls into two sections, one of which is directed to the elaboration and strengthening of the new guild government, the other to the effective taming of the noble brawlers. The latter section, because of the sensational penalties assessed against the insolent miscreants, has in the presentation of many historians completely overshadowed the constitutional section. This is a distinction it does not deserve. For our purpose it suffices to sum it up by saying that on all persons designated by the law as noble an exceptionally heavy money fine was imposed in case of even a minor violence against a member of the common people; in case of a major violence culminating in death the offender was obliged to pay with his life coupled with the destruction of his houses. All that remains to be added is that after a short period of indecision this radical legislation proved so effective that the evil at which it struck completely disappeared.

The more strictly constitutional portion of the Ordinances calls for close attention. The executive functions of the new chief officials, the priors, were more clearly defined as was also the manner of their living together as a single family during their two-month period of office. Other paragraphs dealt with the manner in which the incumbents were to conduct the election of their successors; and a very notable paragraph created a seventh prior who was to be entitled banner-bearer or gonfalonier of Justice and to act as the head and spokesman of his colleagues.

Immediately preceding the enactment of the Ordinances, their champion, Giano della Bella, had provided for the broadening of the guild foundations by adding nine additional minor or craft guilds to the guilds on which the government at that time rested. Consequently, the constitution completed in 1293 listed under their specific names seven major guilds (or arts), five middle guilds, and nine minor guilds, which had the distinction of carrying on their rosters the names of all citizens eligible for the priorate. In point of fact there was so little difference, financial, economic, or otherwise, between the middle and the minor guilds that they were before long lumped together as the fourteen minor guilds, and it is as such that they figure in Florentine history. So far as the wording of the Ordinances went the members of the major and the minor arts enjoyed complete parity in the matter of eligibility to office. However, through the more than two centuries this constitution operated, the priors issued in overwhelming proportion from the greater guilds. In short, whatever the intention of the Ordinances may have been, they worked out in practice as substantially an oligarchic or merchant government.

With the great act of 1293 Florence set a crown on its two-hundred-year-old struggle to break the bonds of the feudal system and achieve the status of a free and sovereign republic. However, while henceforth sovereign, free, and a republic, it was a republic of a peculiar kind. Political rights, as we have seen, were reserved exclusively to the members of the seven major and the fourteen minor guilds and, in spite of a theoretical equality, the major guilds completely dominated their minor fellows. Regardless of these limitations, which were never other than temporarily removed and which demonstrate beyond a doubt that Florence never became a full-fledged democracy, the town nonetheless developed a social atmosphere of a distinctly democratic flavor. Visitors from other Italian cities never failed to be struck with it. Its special merit was that it unified the population as it was unified in no other town of the peninsula and that it promoted a free and easy social intercourse all the way from prosperous merchant to needy beggar, from the highest to the lowest stratum of the population.

II

THE INDEPENDENT REPUBLIC: FROM THE ORDINANCES OF JUSTICE TO THE RISE OF THE MEDICI

WITH the Ordinances of Justice of 1293 Florence provided itself with a republican form of government, to which it then clung with amazing attachment until the tragic overthrow of 1530. These almost two and a half republican centuries embrace the main matter of its history and constitute besides a memorable segment of the story of our Western civilization. The period's outstanding political event was the rise of the Medici, on which account it falls into two sections conveniently labeled Before and After the Medici. Since the agreed concern of this book is the After-the-Medici section, this chapter, which, like its predecessor, proposes no more than to provide the background for the proper understanding of the Medicean developments, will limit itself to a concise review of the leading vicissitudes of the republic between the achievement of the priorate and the Medicean encroachment.

While learning in the preceding chapter of the municipal de-

velopments culminating in the Ordinances of Justice, we also
learned something of the wider provincial developments, more
particularly of how Florence, the stalwart leader of the Guelph
party, had, through the successful repression of its Ghibelline
opponents, achieved an uneasy primacy in Tuscany. How uneasy was made clear by the unbroken succession of wars in which
it became involved in order to maintain its primacy and which
were far from resulting in an unbroken succession of victories.
It will be well to resume our narrative of events with this intra-
provincial struggle, and all the more readily because it never
ceased to be the chief factor in the shaping of the town's policy
to the very end of the republican period.

On reverting to the public happenings that befell immediately
after the establishment of the priorate, let us take note that sharp
on the heels of this domestic event Florence levied war on the
commune of Arezzo on the upper Arno. It resorted to war because Arezzo had overthrown the Guelph regime imposed on
it by Florence and reverted to the outlawed Ghibelline system.
The overturn occurred in 1287 and encouraged Pisa at the
Arno's mouth to follow the Aretine example by casting out the
uncongenial Guelph party and trusting its fortunes once again
to the local Ghibellines. The two co-ordinated occurrences signified a Ghibelline resurgence which Guelph Florence regarded as
a challenge to its supremacy and resolved to meet and scatter
as quickly as possible.

As had been the case from the origin of the communal movement, the wars of the Tuscan towns were still waged at this
time by their citizen militias. Consequently, when Florence mo-
bilized against Arezzo and in 1289 won a smashing victory at
Campaldino, the traditional system was established more firmly
than ever in public esteem. The Pisan campaign that immediately
followed had a different issue, for the Pisans experimented with a
departure from the familiar system by entrusting the conduct
of the war to a professional soldier commanding a body of hired
troops. Against the greater competence of the trained captain

and his mercenaries, the people's army of the Florentines proved
to be helpless and the Pisan campaign ended in failure.

Far from being the first Italian government to professional-
ize war, the Pisans had done no more than copy an innovation
which had made its earliest appearance in northern Italy, in
Lombardy, and then with extraordinary rapidity had pushed its
way down the boot of the peninsula. It requires no elaborate
exposition to show that the popular armies of the emerging communes were from a military angle extremely inefficient. It also
goes without saying that the merchants and shopkeepers who
constituted it were eager to be relieved from the burdensome
service in the field by having the unaccustomed fighting turned
over to a professional hireling troop. True, there were many
drawbacks to the mercenary system but, given over more and
more wholeheartedly to trade and industry, the citizens were
disposed to put up with them rather than suffer the unwelcome
interruption of their normal activities by the recurrent call to
arms.

Probably the worst of the evils connected with the military
innovation was that the commander of mercenaries, usually a
lesser feudal lord, might refuse to take his departure on the
expiration of his contract. He might then cap the argument
that followed by overthrowing the government that employed
him and making himself master. Or, just as likely, a clever and
ambitious local politician might take the mercenary leader under
his wing and with his help toss the popular government into
the discard and raise himself to a throne. It was truly amazing
with what speed the tyrannical trend implicit in the new military system got the upper hand throughout the area of the
originally self-governing communes. As early as the beginning
of the fourteenth century, the transformation was so plainly the
outstanding peninsular phenomenon that the poet Dante, who,
as a young man, had fought in the citizen army that won the
afore-mentioned battle of Campaldino, broke into moving

lament over the hateful change. Listen to what he says of the
altered aspect of the peninsula in the Divine Comedy:

> *For all the towns of Italy are full*
> *Of tyrants, and becometh a Marcellus* [1]
> *Each peasant churl who plays the partisan.*

PURGATORIO, VI, 124-27

On a military usurper clamping his yoke on a free commune he
was called *signore,* signifying lord and master.

Now that Florence proved itself more attached to liberty
and less inclined to the new tyrannical fashion than any other
commune of Italy does not admit of dispute. It is this resolute
frame of mind that constitutes its peculiar distinction and accounts for its undisputed inclusion in the company of the
world's famous republics. The high honor does not however
mean that our town never yielded an inch to tyranny until it
was imposed by the sly, subterranean machinations of Cosimo
de' Medici. That Cosimo, while continuing to wear the mask
of citizen, was the first tyrant ever suffered by Florence has
become part of the town's cherished mythology, with which
the present writer proposes to deal with due respect but without surrendering on that account his professional integrity.

The known and incontestable facts reveal that during the
century that preceded the appearance of the Medici, Florence
repeatedly found itself obliged to come to terms with the new
tyrannical mode. The admittedly involuntary subjection occurred whenever its adoption presented itself as an escape, and
possibly the only escape, from what looked like impending destruction. In spite of the distaste our devotedly republican community felt for the obnoxious new institution, there was no
denying that the concentration of authority in the hands of a
single official, call him signore or what you will, offered a better
prospect of successful resistance to an oncoming host under

---

[1] Marcellus is the Roman general, M. Claudius Marcellus, and symbolizes here the overbearing military leader.

an apparently invincible leader than a multiple executive of priors with an office term of a paltry two months. When we further consider that a war-inured professional captain regularly operated with professional troops, which an untrained, inadequately equipped city militia could not hope successfully to withstand in the field, we will register no surprise that the steady advance of tyranny, of which Dante speaks, was attended by the parallel abandonment of the people's army. To support these statements with the relevant historical facts we shall have to look somewhat more closely into the Florentine developments of the first half of the fourteenth century.

In the year 1310 an emperor descended into Italy with the laughably anachronistic plan of reviving a power which had vanished beyond the chance of recovery with the death, over half a century before, of the exceptionally capable Frederick II. The emperor, Henry VII by name, was a high-minded feudal warrior, to whom, as the Ghibelline banner-bearer, the poet Dante, it will always be remembered, gave an ecstatic welcome. Not so Florence, which a decade before the coming of Henry had driven this same Dante from its midst and had then, on the score of his flaming Ghibelline sentiments, gone the ferocious length of condemning him to death by fire. The rabidly Guelph and anti-imperial town successfully repelled a siege by the claimant to imperial honors, who, not many months after this decisive rebuff, died at Buonconvento in Tuscany from a fever contracted during the campaign.

The unexpected death of Emperor Henry VII spread panic through Ghibelline Pisa, which, having enthusiastically supported the imperial adventurer, was now exposed to the vengeance of the resurgent Guelphs with Florence in their van. Accordingly, the Pisan government looked to its defense by taking into its pay a troop of German cavalry which the death of Henry had deprived of its employer. At the same time it set over them as their captain a Tuscan nobleman and famous swashbuckler, Uguccione della Faggiuola. To curry favor with the Pisan populace, which for centuries had cultivated a savage feud with neighboring Lucca, Uguccione threw himself on this town and captured it. With the backing of the common people, delighted with his capture, he then overthrew the Pisan government by which he was employed and, with Pisa, Lucca, and their respective territories in his hands, towered over Tuscany as its dominant figure and prospective master.

Even before this ominous rise of the Pisan tyrant had occurred, Florence, in preparation for an expected second attack by Emperor Henry VII, had taken a significant step. In return for promised military aid, it invited King Robert of Naples to assume the lordship (*signoria*) over it for a stated number of years. During that period he was to have the right to appoint the podestà without, however, in any respect altering the constitution. Although a strictly limited surrender, it was painful to Florentine pride and was rendered still more painful by failing to meet its purpose; for, while it was Uguccione, and not, as originally expected, the emperor who took the field against Florence, when in August, 1315, the two battle arrays clashed at Montecatini, Uguccione drove the Florentines in wild rout from the field.

Since nothing was more unstable than the regimes of the rank crop of military adventurers who for the next two centuries overshadowed the Italian scene, it should not surprise us that, before the victorious lord of Pisa could do further injury to Florence, he was tripped and brought to fall by his young lieutenant, Castruccio Castracane. Although serving the lord of Pisa, Castruccio's home town was Lucca, with the capture of which Uguccione had begun his career of conquest. Since the rebel upstart succeeded to Uguccione's undiminished authority, the transfer of tyranny brought no relief to Florence. However, arms rested for a number of years until Castruccio, unable longer to restrain his ambitious nature, suddenly pounced upon and captured Pistoia. This town lay so close to Florence that its seizure practically planted the young tyrant on the Arno city's doorstep. Put thus in genuine jeopardy, the alarmed Florentines resolved to drive the aggressor off with a superhuman military effort. It proved an unqualified disaster, for when in September, 1325, the Florentine army encountered Castruccio's forces at Altopascio, it suffered an even worse rout than at Montecatini ten years before.

Need we be surprised that in their dejection and despair the priors once again resorted to the device of the tyrant? Since the contract of surrender to King Robert of Naples had not been renewed when, in the year 1322, it had run its stipulated course, Florence had again become free. But when, in 1325, after the Altopascio overthrow, the city, temporarily stripped of defenders, faced the triumphant Castruccio, it again, and with panicky alacrity, took shelter under the wing of Naples by accepting King Robert's son and heir, the duke of Calabria, as its master. While conceding to the duke much greater powers than it had, on the earlier occasion, granted to his father, it made a similar provision for the ultimate resumption of its ever cherished independence by limiting the duke's control to a term of ten years. Nonetheless, with or without limitation, the town had again surrendered its independence. Three years later the new tyranny was providentially terminated by two happy, interlocking events. These were the practically simultaneous deaths of Castruccio, the aggressor tyrant of Lucca, and the duke of Calabria, his Florentine counterpart.

That brings us to the third and by far the most complete and humiliating of the city's experiments with the form of government which was progressively imposing itself on the whole peninsula. It came about under pressure of an extraordinarily complicated set of circumstances which will have to be sternly condensed to be fitted into our abbreviated account of the Florentine happenings of this period. We shall content ourselves to indicate the episode's two leading causative streams. One had its source in the dark vicissitudes of war, the other in the even darker and more impenetrable vicissitudes of business and finance. Familiar by now with the uninterrupted flow of war through and over Tuscany, we shall trace first this particular line of causation and register no surprise on learning that, immediately on Castruccio's death, the Lucchese state, his very personal creation, went disastrously to pieces. Under the eternal seesaw among the towns of Tuscany contending for supremacy, it was now the turn of Florence to take the offensive and, if possible, to capture Lucca. And this was the precise project the Arno city formed but could not bring to a successful head by reason of the jealous intervention of the neighbor governments, firmly resolved to balk Florence of its prey. Even the two powerful tyrant families of Lombardy, the Visconti and the Scala, who had set up their powerful regimes in Milan and Verona respectively, took a hand in the game.

With astonishing persistence Florence clung for years to its plan of conquest, only to have Lucca, in July, 1342, fall victim at long last to the rival Pisans. Half crazed with rage and disappointment, the city resolved as a final desperate measure to try its luck against its leagued enemies with a military adventurer. This was the Frenchman, Count Walter of Brienne, who commonly appears in the public records of the period under the courtesy title of duke of Athens. His leading, perhaps his only, recommendation in Florentine eyes was that he was related by marriage to that Neapolitan dynasty to which, on the approach of danger, Florence had already twice before surrendered its liberty. The precise call issued to Count Walter was to serve as captain general of the town's armed forces. But no sooner had he arrived at Florence than he resolved to overthrow the government of the priors which had hired him and make himself tyrant. The traditional meeting of the people in the public square, the parlamentum, had never been formally abolished. Learning of this obsolete tool from one of his legal advisers, Count Walter resolved to employ it in order to achieve his purpose. On September 8, 1342, he had the people summoned to the piazza by the ringing of the great town-bell and so skill-

fully played his game that they urged him with wild shouts of
a vita, a vita to take over the rule of their city for the term of
his life.

Since nothing precisely like this had ever happened in the
city before, the episode, carrying the name of Count Walter,
has always figured conspicuously in the Florentine record. However, in spite of intense research, its hidden origins have to such
an extent eluded disclosure that many contradictory theories
have been, and still are, entertained regarding them. Quite the
most plausible conjecture ties up Walter of Brienne's usurpation
with the contemporary financial crisis and obliges us, if we are to
grasp the issue, to set forth the economic developments of the
Arno city which ran parallel to the succession of military events.

Florentine merchant enterprise has been accepted by the historians of every school as the fundamental factor in the growth
and expansion of the city. It is also agreed among them that it
brought with it economic practices identified with the system
commonly called capitalism. An absorbing feature of the rising capitalism of Florence was that, in spite of its youth, it
already exhibited all the characteristics attending it through the
ages, more particularly the regular and incurable pendulum
swing between "boom" and "depression." As recorded in the
previous chapter, the city's first great boom gave the merchant
class such a grip on the town that it was able to carry through
the political revolution of 1282 associated with the name of
the priors. A second, mightier boom began some twenty years
later and greatly increased the merchant prosperity by the vast
enlargement of the woolen trade. Let it, for clarity's sake, be
repeated that the distribution over Europe of Florentine woolen
cloth was managed by merchant companies and that these companies, very early in their history, found it advantageous to
combine with their merchandising activity the varied business
of a bank.

By the beginning of the fourteenth century it had come
about that the larger Florentine merchant companies, such as

the Bardi and the Peruzzi, did much of the banking business of the western world. Evidence thereof is their leading role as money-lenders to the sovereigns of France and England. Early swollen profits in this field led them, like innumerable successors after them, to overplay their hand; for when the two western monarchies inaugurated the conflict that has gone down in history as the Hundred Years' War, the money-minded Florentine banking houses undertook to finance both sides. On thus carelessly sowing the wind, they promptly reaped the whirlwind. In 1339, only a few years after launching his attack on France, King Edward III of England defaulted on his interest payments and, shortly after, repudiated his debts altogether. There immediately followed a run on the Florentine banks. It would have speedily ended in a general collapse, had not government and creditors considerately granted a moratorium. However, henceforward the banks rested on such shaky foundations that their proprietors kept eagerly searching the horizon for signs of relief. Instead of relief, it was a new storm that broke over them. It struck when the government of their own city, immersed to its throat in the heaped expenditures of the endless Lucchese war, deepened the crisis by in its turn suspending payment on its loans. Made panicky by the savage mutterings of the unemployed and starving workers against them and the whole ruling merchant class, the bankers evolved the hazardous plan of escaping ruin by having recourse to a tyrant. Owing his elevation to their favor, they might flatter themselves that he would save their threatened fortunes by conducting his office in their interest.

The sly intrigue went astray for the sufficient reason that the tyrant imported by the banking houses resolved to play not their game but his own. If it was bankers who brought Count Walter to Florence, it was himself who fathered the scheme of having himself made signore by the action of the Florentine masses. Consequently, insofar as his admittedly low intelligence permitted him consistently to follow a program, he resolved to favor the disfranchised mass of the woolen workers to which he owed his elevation to his post of tyrant. But this was tantamount to promoting revolution and quickly turned into active enemies not only his original sponsors of the greater guilds but also the far more numerous shopkeepers of the lesser guilds. The upshot might have been foreseen. Less than a year after his installation in the Palazzo Pubblico he was driven ignominiously from the town.

Although the government of the priors, which had by now taken deep root in the Florentine consciousness, was re-established, it was not set up again without a change. Ever since the passage of the Ordinances of Justice, the power in the state, as we are aware, rested theoretically with the twenty-one guilds. In point of fact, however, it had, practically without interruption, been appropriated by means of cunningly veiled manipulations by the seven greater guilds. Under their self-appointed guidance the town had amazingly prospered, the personal wealth of the manipulators had vastly increased, and even the woolen workers, who constituted the bulk of the population but who, forbidden by law to form guilds, enjoyed no political rights, had been benefited to the extent at least of finding the regular employment which provided them and their families with bread.

The prolonged financial crisis of 1339-1343 put a stop to this development, for it brought with it a veritable landslide of business failures attended by shattering unemployment. The obvious reaction of the suffering population was to blame the collapse on the merchant oligarchs, and so great and general was the resentment against them that the demand was voiced which in comparable present-day crises issues in the cry of "turn the rascals out." However, nothing so drastic resulted from the Florentine crisis of 1343, for it terminated with nothing more sweeping than the reduction of the influence of the greater guilds in the crucial office of the priors and with a corresponding increase in the representation of the lesser guilds. Such was the slight substance of the political reform effected on the expulsion of Count Walter of Brienne. While it certainly cannot be considered to have constituted a radical revolution, it did inaugurate an interlude of about forty years, during which the leading domestic issue agitating the commonwealth took the form of a struggle for control between the great merchants and the common people, between oligarchy and democracy.

Not for a single moment after its victory was the reformed government with its larger representation of the crafts free from harassment by the greater guilds. The merchant oligarchs simply would not abandon the hope of regaining the full measure of their lost supremacy. And in point of fact by the tricky devices in which they were adept, they made such steady headway that the slowly gathering resentment of the cheated little folk culminated at last in the greatest domestic disturbance of Florentine history. It is commonly called the Revolt of the Ciompi. The word *ciompi* had come into circulation some years before as a popular designation for the woolen workers, who were the recipients at best of starvation wages and who, as we have already heard, were forbidden by law to attempt to improve their lot by organizing as guilds.

The Revolt of the Ciompi occurred in the summer of 1378 and followed immediately on the heels of a more circumscribed revolt carried through by the lesser guilds prompted and abetted by some sympathetic members of the greater guilds. These latter, deserters from their own class, had gone over to the craftsmen because they were outraged no less than their humbler countrymen by the dark intrigues and devious methods whereby the greater guilds had again got control into their hands. Gonfalonier of Justice, and therefore titular head of the priors for the bimestrial period of May-June, 1378, was Salvestro de' Medici, who, though himself an outstanding merchant oligarch, sided with the wronged craftsmen. In June, just before the expiration of his term, he gave the sign for a popular rising against the group of plotting oligarchs who did their nefarious work obscurely in the dark but whose impressive persons were familiar to everybody. As is not unusual in such affairs the demonstration got out of hand and, before the day was over, the excited mob had entered and sacked the houses of the oligarchic leaders and driven the leaders themselves in tumultuous flight from the city. Immediately afterward, Salvestro de' Medici passed out of office and, so far as he and his craftsmen allies were concerned, the revolution was over.

But it was not over because the convulsive disturbance of the social atmosphere caused the disfranchised mass of the woolworkers, the ciompi, to catch fire and continue the street demonstrations in their own behalf. They poured into the piazza in irresistible waves demanding that they be accorded the right to organize guilds in order that by this decisive concession they, too, might at long last participate in the government. When the timid new gonfalonier of Justice tried to put the petitioners off with crooked words, the angered multitude broke into the palace and, flooding it with their numbers, obliged the priors to run for their lives. The upshot of the savage disturbance was that the woolworkers were granted the right to organize two guilds of their own. By adding these new units to the constitutionally established fourteen lesser guilds, the humbler elements of the population reached a total of sixteen guilds against the seven guilds of the more prosperous citizens. Strengthened in numbers and elated, besides, by their successful revolution, the common people found themselves, as the total result of the riotous year of 1378, in possession of the preponderant power in the government.

The preponderance was so indecisive and under such uninterrupted attack by the merchant element that it lasted a bare three years. What weakened it from the start, and in the end fatally, was the open hostility between the shopkeepers and woolworkers lumped together in the same broad category of lesser arts. Neither in the fourteenth nor in any later century have the small bourgeoisie and the industrial workers found it easy to merge their interests; and so sharp was the division between the two classes in Florence that shopkeeper opinion was almost as savagely opposed to its new associates as were the oligarchs of the greater guilds. Besides, precisely as throughout the previous hundred years, the merchants held obdurately to the view that the government of the city was their god-given prerogative and never ceased weaving plots to re-establish themselves in power. They were, let us always remember, not only merchants but also, owing to the peculiar Florentine developments, industrialists and employers of labor. By the time the year 1382 was rung in they felt themselves strong enough to go into action. By a sudden attack, which they entrusted to hired soldiers, on the woolworkers in their crowded slums they brought them to submission and, then, by a special legislative act had the charters of the two proletarian guilds revoked. It is possible that in this upsurge of power they might have succeeded in revoking also the charters of the original fourteen craft guilds. However, they were too prudent to entertain so extreme a measure and were mindful besides that the lesser guilds had, on the whole, been always properly submissive to their betters. Consequently, they confirmed to these old associates of theirs the modest share in the offices they had enjoyed before the first rising against the greater guilds some forty years earlier.

The merchant oligarchy, which in 1382 broke and all but smothered the democratic movement, was not again displaced as long as Florence enjoyed an unbroken political existence. Even the rule of the Medici, although called a tyranny and undoubtedly possessed of some of its aspects, was essentially nothing other than a later aspect of the oligarchy which took over the government in the above-named year. While this prolonged exercise of power very definitely resulted from the continued subjection in which the merchant element succeeded in keeping the two far more numerous classes of the shopkeepers and the woolen workers, another factor belonging to the field of foreign affairs came powerfully to the aid of the triumphant system. Let us therefore have a look at a development in general peninsular politics which pushed to the front in the second half of the fourteenth century.

By that time the prolonged inter-communal strife had either led, or was rapidly leading, to the absorption of the many small communes into a few relatively powerful ones. A wide-awake, intelligent Florentine citizen, whom we may imagine surveying the peninsula about the time the oligarchs swamped the democratic elements, could not fail to have been struck with this movement that had taken place toward peninsular consolidation. What he would have noted was that two vigorous states had come to dominate the area to the north of his city and two equally vigorous states the area to its south. The two northern giants—an inflated but permissible figure of speech if we limit our outlook to Italy—were Milan and Venice, the former a duchy under the Visconti dynasty, the latter a merchant republic; the two southern giants were Naples, a kingdom, and the States of the Church, a heterogeneous mass of minor tyrannies loosely gathered together under the sovereignty of the pope. If Florence thought highly enough of its importance to enter into competition with these four superior polities, it would have to imitate their methods and aim to bring Tuscany into subjection to itself in order to command the resources of a roughly equivalent territorial mass. As we know, the town had, practically from its origin, struggled to establish its authority over Tuscany and had more than once come within sight of its objective. However, every past advance had again been canceled by a setback, the most recent of these reversals having occurred in the time of Walter of Brienne. During his tyranny practically every town, large or small, which had already made submission to Florence, reasserted its independence. The result was that when, on the expulsion of Walter, the government of the priors was revived, the most pressing problem with which it was confronted had been to bring the rebels back to obedience.

Since the humble folk, who in the democratically influenced

period of 1343-1382 exercised a measure of control, were as fervently devoted to the greatness of Florence as their oligarchic rivals, it may fairly be said of them that they let no opportunity slip to draw Tuscany again within their net. They scored some minor successes, but, because of the continuing internal divisions, were not able to pursue a steady and unwavering course. It thus came about that when, in 1382, the merchant oligarchs returned to power, the work of subduing the larger towns of Tuscany remained still to be done. An oligarchy, especially if under the direction of an intelligent ruling junta, is much more likely than a contentious democracy resolutely to pursue a policy of territorial expansion. The judgment receives confirmation from the successes piled up by the particular oligarchy here under review. Only two years after taking over the government it gained possession of Arezzo on the upper Arno; and some twenty years later it fulfilled an ambition the Florentines had entertained for more than a century by the capture of the coastal city of Pisa. Except for Lucca and Siena, which eluded every attempt to bring them into the fold, Florence under the oligarchy made itself master in Tuscany and by this enlargement gained a sufficient territorial base to figure as a fifth Italian power on an approximate level with the other four, with Milan, Venice, Naples, and the pope.

The Florentine territorial consolidation took place in the nick of time; for certain of its Italian rivals, first Milan and, later, Naples, were moved under warlike rulers to attempt to extend their territories, more particularly in the direction of Tuscany; and if Florence had not taken it upon itself to defeat these attacks delivered, luckily for the Arno city, not simultaneously but with a peace-time interval between them, Tuscany might have been incorporated in either a north or a south Italian state. Obliged for years to conduct defensive campaigns against the Milanese and Neapolitan despots, Florence was repeatedly on the verge of succumbing to the better equipment and more effective strategy of its opponents. In point of fact it was, in every instance, saved from threatened destruction by the fortunate sudden death of its tormentor, and so had Lady Luck and not its own prowess to thank for its delivery. However, since it was undeniable that the city had repeatedly escaped from imminent peril during the regime of the oligarchs, the glory of the rescue accrued to them. It continued to envelop them like an aura until, in an evil hour, they resolved that the time had come once more to attempt the conquest of the ever elusive Lucca. Their renewed failure in this enterprise led to their overthrow—a story we will adjourn until we have had a look at their conduct of domestic affairs.

A second observation on oligarchies, the validity of which is confirmed by countless instances, is that their strength depends on their unbroken unity. While it is true that every oligarchy is perpetually threatened by the groups it has deprived of political power, a more immediate danger to its ascendancy arises from a split among the rulers themselves. It is the uncurbed ambition of individual leaders and the consequent hidden struggle among them for control that has in innumerable historical cases drawn an oligarchy onward to its destruction. The Florentine oligarchy dating from the year 1382 made a fortunate start by falling under a leader who, by combining firmness with flexibility, secured it a long lease of life. He convincingly disclosed his firmness by halting at no measure, no matter how raw and unscrupulous, to rid himself of a rival seemingly set on following an individual course. His no less notable flexibility appeared in his readiness to share the rule with associates who, while commending themselves by their talents, showed themselves amenable to discipline and did not kick over the party traces.

This exceptional oligarch was Maso degli Albizzi and it is owing to his genius that the revived merchant rule carries the Albizzi label. By taking capable men like Gino Capponi and Niccolò da Uzzano into partnership with himself, Maso degli Albizzi's control took on the appearance more of a closely bound junta than that of a single leader of the kind familiar to

us in America under the name of "boss." The exceptional Maso
died in 1417 and, shortly after, was followed in death by Gino
Capponi. That left in control Niccolò da Uzzano, definitely one
of the outstanding personages of the age. To confirm this judgment it will suffice to have a look at the colored terra cotta bust
of him, molded by Donatello's master hand. Niccolò showed his
kindly disposition by promptly admitting his friend Maso's son,
Rinaldo degli Albizzi, into political partnership with himself.

Rinaldo degli Albizzi was a high-spirited young man, who
believed in strong measures and could defend them at need with
a striking native eloquence. Gradually pushing his cautious and
ageing associate aside, he adopted a headlong policy which presently had the ship of state floundering in heavy seas. In 1422 he
became involved in war with Filippo Maria, duke of Milan. For
this he can hardly be blamed, for the successive dukes of Milan
for some generations past had by their rage for conquest figured
as the perennial disturbers of the peninsula's peace. Nor can it
fairly be laid at his door that the war with the Milanese tyrant
proved a grueling and exhausting contest which was not brought
to a close till after six costly campaigns. However, it can incon-
testably be charged against him that, no sooner had the Milanese
war been concluded than he threw himself on Lucca, thereby
inaugurating the latest in a long series of efforts to add that
town, together with its territory, to the Florentine dominion.

The Lucchese war was begun in 1429 and through bungling
diplomacy and flagrant mismanagement in the field attributable
in large measure to Rinaldo in person, was attended by an unbroken string of fiascos. Nonetheless Rinaldo refused to let go.
He was committed to his course in the first instance by the
people of Florence themselves who, roused to a passionate patriotism, had set their hearts on at last reducing their stubborn
western neighbor to subjection. But when campaign after campaign came to the same futile end, public opinion turned sharply
against Rinaldo not, let it be understood, because he had embarked on a brutal war of conquest but because his policy had

not been crowned with success. There followed the kind of domestic crisis which, since the beginning of time, has put war-making governments in imminent peril. Rinaldo was obliged to face a mounting tide of criticism which tended to crystallize around his leading opponent. This was Cosimo, head of the Medici family. It thus came about that the disastrous Lucchese war precipitated a personal conflict between Rinaldo degli Albizzi, resolved to retain the leading position in the state which he owed to the oligarchic regime fashioned by his father, and Cosimo de' Medici who, though not a member of the ruling clique, had risen into view as the richest banker of the town.

At this point we bring our hurried review of the early republican centuries of Florentine history to a close. To understand how the head-on collision between Rinaldo and Cosimo was resolved, we shall have to become acquainted with the Medici family and Cosimo's rise to the position of leader of the oligarchic opposition. However, we shall not follow this lead at once. Before embarking on the story of the Medici, the agreed subject matter of this book, we shall have to take time out to support a declaration coupled with our original statement of purpose. That declaration was that, long before the Medici made their bid for political mastery, Florence had given birth to a promising native culture and carried it to an amazing richness of expression.

III

THE PRE-MEDICEAN STAGES OF
FLORENTINE CULTURE

NOTHING is better established regarding human societies
than that their culture is the product of their adventuring spirit and has its deepest root in religion. This is certainly
true of the culture of Florence and explains why its earliest
fruits appeared when the town, floating on a tide of faith, experienced the economic and political revival associated with the
communal rebirth of the eleventh century. While the most immediately apparent consequence of the revival was the enjoyment by the citizens of more abundant goods and their bolder
attack on the feudal straitjacket which cramped their movements, a more concealed but no less lively effect was a strengthened attachment to God and his saints to whose favor the blessings so bountifully showered on the town were gladly attributed.

It was inevitable that the desire to give thanks to the heavenly
benefactors should be directed to the adornment of the existing churches. They were for the most part laid out on an
exceedingly small scale and miserably furnished. Their improvement, attended by the erection of larger and handsomer edifices,

would reflect not only the deepened devotion of the worshipers but would serve in addition to display the mounting dignity of the young commune. As early as the first half of the eleventh century, at a time therefore when the commune had not yet fully awakened from its medieval slumbers, a Florentine bishop erected the church of San Miniato on the lovely hill to the east of the town substantially in the form in which it presents itself to view today. It was the isolated act of a great prelate and was not followed by a comparable ecclesiastical structure for many generations to come. For Florentines and admiring foreigners alike it is a pleasant thought that storied San Miniato is the earliest exhibit in the stately pageantry of art unrolled by the Arno town in the course of the next five centuries.

It is the sincere practice of the simple and immemorial crafts that throughout the course of history has been found to underlie the development of the arts; and Florence is no exception to the rule. Florentine art had its beginning in the ornamental elaboration of articles of use connected with the service of the altars. Among them were chalices for the wine of the mass, pyxes for the consecrated host, embossed and jeweled reliquaries for the bones of saints and other sacred remains. From these works of limited scope the craftsmen gradually passed to more ambitious projects, such as stone or marble constructions framing the altar-table and the sculptured figures and painted images of the particular saints to whom the altars were dedicated. In this manner, over the desire to make more beautiful the house of God and multiply for the greater edification of the worshipers the symbols of the faith, did the arts come to an ever mounting fullness of expression.

In the two to three hundred years that lie between the birth of the arts and the rise of the Medici the arts passed through several phases which it is the purpose of this chapter to set forth. Committed by our Introduction to the position that the Florentines owed the treasure of their arts to their own genius, we are now faced with the necessity of tracing, however briefly, the developments in this field antecedent to the Medici.

But the arts, whether major or minor, whether the so-called Fine Arts or the lesser crafts, are by no means the only spiritual value to which the genius of the young commune gave birth. A large segment of its achievement is concerned with literature and thought, which, because of their close interaction, may profitably be linked together. It will therefore be our task to indicate also the pre-Medicean literature and thought to which Florence gave expression; and since they are no less important than the arts and in some ways more immediately revealing of the spirit underlying them, it is with literature and thought that we shall begin our cultural review.

Our city of Florence had no share in the intellectual activity of the Middle Ages which revolved chiefly about theology and philosophy and carries the name of scholasticism. Arising, not as an ecclesiastical but as a trading center, the town directed its awakening intellectual curiosity to the immediately pressing problems of public and private conduct. In other words, it turned to the Here and away from the Hereafter, which was the chosen land of the scholastic doctors. By this shift of attention a movement of worldliness or secularization took its place by the side of the prescriptive contemplation of the Heavenly City and gradually overshadowed it. The most striking consequence of this trend was the closer scrutiny by the townsmen of the world in which they lived coupled with the desire to reduce their slowly accumulating items of information concerning it to a clarifying and intelligible order.

The first Florentine to illustrate the slowly growing secular quality of native thought was Brunetto Latini, who lived in the second half of the thirteenth century. It helps account for his worldly bent that he was a lawyer by profession who rose to the high post of chancellor of the republic. His broadly intellectual, as distinct from his narrowly professional, interest was manifested by his founding a school for boys which was attended by the youthful Dante. However, what chiefly signalizes his importance in the history of thought was his production of a kind of primitive encyclopedia called *Il Tesoro* (the Treasure). While it rates in our eyes as no better than a hodge-podge of idle gossip and superstition, its announced purpose was to provide his ignorant countrymen with a convenient compendium of knowledge on a strictly secular level. It is therefore, in spite of its uncritical chatter, a pioneering work.

On turning next to Latini's pupil, to Dante, we are confronted with the exceptional case of the genius who cannot be fitted into any fixed scheme of cultural development. While Dante, like Latini, swam in the novel stream of secular thought, he was far more happily and intensely at home in the traditional stream identified with the medieval doctors. Consequently, his fame in his own time rested, and in ours still rests, on the imposing poem, wherein he reached the unique distinction of lifting the Christian plan of salvation out of the abstruse world of theology into the sensuous and imaginative world of poetry. With his matchless *Divine Comedy* he faced backward toward the medieval ideology which in his time had already begun to evaporate. It is on this account that his great work has often been called the Swan Song of the Middle Ages. But every reader sensitive to intellectual change will hail it with equal conviction as the Lark Song of the Modern Age; for no poet has ever lived who was more deeply steeped than Dante in the immediate impressions of the world of sense, ranked by medieval orthodoxy as the perilous realm of Satan.

In the light of the *Divine Comedy*, therefore, Dante is both a medieval and a modern man. But, sanctified poet that he preeminently was, he was also a Florentine citizen and shared with his fellow townsmen all the interests that engrossed them. Consequently, like Latini before him, he was a seeker after mundane knowledge and in witness of this interest, began but did not finish a Tesoro of his own, called *Il Convivio* (the Banquet). It is, of course, a completely negligible work compared with the illuminated vision of man's destiny projected by the *Divine Comedy;* but there it is.

The double stimulus emanating from Dante resulted in two memorable movements, which, though distinct, are yet related. The first concerns the rise and spread of Italian literature, the second the intensification of the new mundane interest until it blossomed into the intellectual revolution commonly called humanism. It was Francesco Petrarch on whom the two-fold mantle of Dante descended. By his lyric poetry, especially by his moving sonnets addressed to Madonna Laura, he gave new luster to the literary movement inaugurated by his inspired predecessor and by directing the as yet blind and groping secular interest to the diminished but still considerable body of the surviving classical writings he introduced it to a priceless treasure of tested human experience. Petrarch was succeeded by Boccaccio, a man of lesser stature but, like Petrarch, both poet and scholar. While as poet he opened up some new fields of expression, particularly that of the pastoral epic, it was pre-eminently as author in prose of the hundred tales assembled under the title, *The Decameron,* that he gained his literary immortality. Petrarch and Boccaccio, together with their majestic forerunner of the *Divine Comedy,* form the brilliant three-star constellation that presides over the birth of Italian literature. And let it not escape our attention that the career of the three luminaries fell within the fourteenth century, during which the unresolved struggle of the townsmen for an effectively organized and independent republic was at its height.

Important as is the first great outburst of Italian literature, from the loftier viewpoint of European civilization it yields in significance to the secularizing movement that came to a head in humanism. If Petrarch is universally celebrated as the father of humanism, he owes this honor to the fact that it was he who put an end to the hesitant attitude of the generation that preceded him and resolutely turned his back on the outmoded intellectual matter of the medieval schools. There is nothing mysterious about his embarking on this pioneering role. Exposed from birth to the subtly secularizing influence emanating from the prospering towns, he was amazed to discover an outlook closely related to his own in the surviving writings of the Latin authors. That, as is still often avowed, they had been contemptuously pushed aside by the learned doctors of the Middle Ages is not true; but it is certain that, in respect of their essential message, they were not understood by these same doctors because read by them through distorting scholastic glasses. By tossing these obscuring media aside Petrarch came into direct view of the ancient writers and was stirred to unbounded enthusiasm by the striking relevance of their thought to the urban problems that in his time had everywhere in Italy come to the front but nowhere more engrossingly than at Florence.

The feature shared by all the outstanding original contributors to Latin literature was that they had concerned themselves pre-eminently with man and man's lot on earth. This made them humanists and defined their common intellectual background as humanism. Of this classical humanism Petrarch made himself the fiery and intelligently directed champion, since he recognized that the measure preliminary to the successful establishment among his countrymen of the humanistic frame of mind was a systematic revival of ancient literature and learning. It thus came about that humanism and the revival of learning became, and have remained, practically synonymous terms, although it should not be overlooked that humanism or, as in the perspective of the centuries we may call it, progressive secularization, is the wider movement and the revival of learning merely the means employed for the promotion of humanism in the transition period between the Medieval and the Modern Age.

Examined as a movement of classical revival, the activities of Petrarch and the large and enthusiastic following of disciples that promptly gathered around him were directed at very definite goals. The earliest purpose of the band was to multiply for the benefit of the reading public all the extant manuscripts of

Latin literature. Improved acquaintance with the Latin works pointed the way to the literature of the Greeks, from whom, it presently appeared, the Latin authors had in large part derived both their form and their matter. This invaluable broadening of outlook was not effected until a generation after Petrarch's death. The event can be precisely dated by reference to the first Greek language course conducted in Italy. It was instituted at Florence in the year 1396 by a group of local humanists, who engaged for that purpose a learned and personally attractive Greek visitor, Chrysoloras by name. The eager importation of Greek manuscripts followed with their multiplication, largely in Latin translation, soon rivaling that of the Latin works. Coupled with this activity went the feverish search for lost works and the studious collation of the existing copies of the same work for the detection of the errors due to careless medieval scribes and, ultimately, for the re-establishment, as far as possible, of the correct original text.

By these various activities there was gradually staked off an entirely new field of study. Its name is classical philology, which by the labor of scores of devotees was pursued under scholarly norms of a steadily increasing severity. The leading contributor to this development in the generation after Petrarch was the Florentine, Coluccio Salutati (d. 1406). In the generation after Salutati a veritable galaxy of scholars made their appearance with perhaps Leonardo Bruni (d. 1444) and Poggio Bracciolini (d. 1459) giving off the brightest light.

Inevitably from this eager steeping of themselves in pagan thought the humanists gradually took over many of its characteristics, although it was only slowly and to the end never in large numbers that they divested themselves in its entirety of their Christian faith. Inevitably, also, they were moved to press on from scholarship to self-expression and to try their skill at the ancient literary forms with which they had become familiar. Their success in this respect was less than mediocre—a failure without doubt ascribable primarily to their insufficient natural endowment but due also, in part at least, to their rejection of their mother tongue as their literary medium in favor of a foreign language. For that is what the so highly prized Latin in simple truth was, and all the devoted and concentrated attention they gave to its mastery did not avail to cause it to drop easily and naturally from their lips or pens.

The greatest success the humanists achieved in the matter of the revival of forgotten literary forms was in history. The aforementioned Bruni and Poggio composed each a history of Florence modeled as closely as possible on their classical forerunners. But by borrowing both the form and the language of the Romans they produced essentially imitative works which fail to come alive. A hundred years before their time Giovanni Villani had written in his spicy native Tuscan a chronicle of the city of his birth which, although it lacks the indispensable unity of a true history, makes incomparably better reading than the ponderous learned products of his two humanist successors.

Every intellectual advance is as good as certain to carry a measure of loss along with its more memorable profit. The profit of the revival of learning is writ large on the face not only of Italian but also of European culture. It may be epitomized as a leveling of the stifling medieval barriers to afford a deepened backward view of antiquity and, through the stimulus of antiquity, the achievement of a broadened understanding of the contemporary world. In short, the revival of learning traced, for better for worse, the path taken by the new and slowly ripening Western civilization. But, let it not be forgotten, it failed to give birth to an important original literature; indeed, so far as Italy is concerned, by reason of the obsessive attachment of its intellectual elite to the Latin language, it administered a setback to the recently evolved Italian literary movement from which it did not recover for several generations.

It was not until the revival of learning had become a vigorous movement driving forward along the several lines traced by the preceding hurried sketch that the Medici made their entrance on the Florentine stage. Their first outstanding representative was Cosimo, who with his lively intellectual interests lost no time in bringing his liberal patronage to bear on the revival movement. It well deserves and will in due course receive attention in this book. But in view of the fact that the revival of learning became a powerful influence through the nursing efforts of many dedicated spirits anterior to Cosimo, it is plainly contrary to fact to ascribe an originating role to him and his family.

We turn now to Florentine architecture, sculpture, and painting, the so-called Fine Arts, which came to birth as a flowering of the sincere practice of the simpler and more immediately useful crafts. Having already asserted in general terms that the Fine Arts had gone far on their way before the coming of the Medici, we are now obliged to substantiate this claim by marshaling the concrete evidence in its support. Giving architecture the precedence over its sister skills which it commonly receives, we shall propound the following question: What outstanding structures in the greatly expanded and modernized, but still essentially unchanged, Florence of our day go back to the republican period of the thirteenth and fourteenth centuries? All such structures will indisputably be pre-Medicean, since it is not until we come to the fifteenth century that we have to reckon with a possible influence emanating from the famous family.

The most compendious and conclusive way of answering our question is to ascend to the top of the centrally located campanile in order to let our eyes wander freely over the city spread beneath our feet. Once on that lofty lookout, we shall not be long in discovering that the most conspicuous monuments meeting the eye definitely antedate the later rulers of the city. To begin with the campanile itself on which we are standing—it is familiarly called the tower of Giotto and its foundations were laid by that master in the year 1334. Immediately contiguous to the campanile rises the vast mass of the cathedral of Santa Maria del Fiore begun in 1296 and so gradually brought to completion that its crowning feature, the far-seen cupola of Brunelleschi, was not finished till 1434, the very year of the advent to power of Cosimo de' Medici. This makes it clear and indisputable that Cosimo can have had nothing to do with either the planning or the slow and frequently interrupted construction of the great episcopal seat.

Looking westward from our dizzy platform we readily single out the Dominican church of Santa Maria Novella and the many monastic structures gathered under its wing. The foundation of Santa Maria Novella goes back to 1283. It antedates by twelve years the founding of Santa Croce, the church of the rival Franciscan order and plainly visible from our lookout directly to the east. In the same quarter of the heavens but closer at hand rises the slender bell-tower of the old abbey church of La Badia. The existing church may be completely ignored, since it is a conventional seventeenth century replacement of a much earlier original. Fortunately, on the occasion of that ruthless renovation, the graceful Gothic tower, erected in 1330, was left untouched. The tall, cube-shaped building to the south, almost directly under our feet, is Or San Michele. It was erected as a storage house for grain, but its ground floor was from the start reserved as a shrine to house the elaborate marble altar of Orcagna completed in 1359.

Older than the oldest of these monuments and generally given preference over them by discriminating critics of the arts is the baptistery of San Giovanni, which faces the cathedral to the west. Although by universal consent the most ancient monument of the city, its precise date is in dispute among the experts. We shall content ourselves with noting that they are in agreement on just two matters: that San Giovanni is not, as the native tradition obstinately avers, a converted temple of the pagan wargod, Mars, and that it was built *ab origine* as a Christian church somewhere between the fifth and the seventh centuries.

Having from our lofty platform singled out the leading ecclesiastical structures of the pre-Medicean period, let us now cast about for the oldest witnesses of the unfolding civic activities. Our conscientious dating may by now have become extremely boring to our readers but, once committed to the chronological approach, we shall have to carry it through. Eastward, in the direction of Santa Croce, our eye encounters a rude mass of stone terminating in a correspondingly rude tower. It once served as the palace of the podestà and, in a later absolutist age, as the residence of the chief police official, from whose title it was renamed the *Bargello*. Erected between 1250 and 1260, it is the proud monumental reminder of the First Democracy (il primo populo). Not far away leaps, like the spike of a giant lily, the tower of the palace of the priors, the honored executive officials of the proud republican period. Florentines now commonly call it *Palazzo Vecchio* (the Old Palace). While the whole immense structure was for many decades in gradual process of erection, its foundation stone dates from as early as the year 1299. At the foot of the Palazzo Vecchio the *Loggia dei Lanzi* extends a generous welcome to native-born and foreigners alike in three majestic arches of wide span. It was completed in 1382 and was at that time called the *Loggia dei Signori,* since it served as the formal setting for the ceremonious induction into office of the ruling officials, the above-mentioned priors. Of the four bridges across the Arno the oldest and most famous, the bridge with shops called *Ponte Vecchio,* goes back to Roman times. The other three bridges belong to the first half of the thirteenth century. But it must not be understood that any of the four appear in the same vestment of stone with which they were originally clothed. Destructive inundations have repeatedly demolished them only to be more solidly rebuilt on each occasion by the undiscouraged citizens.

A civic structure which once caused the breasts of the citizens to swell with inordinate pride no longer in our day meets the eye. This was the mighty ring of stone which, built between 1284 and 1328 and called the third circle, once girdled the city.

A hundred years ago it still stood with its fifteen massive gates and seventy-three protective towers lining the battlements; but in the second half of the nineteenth century it was removed because it had become an obstruction to traffic and, also, because, in an age of giant artillery, it no longer possessed even a faint trace of defensive value.

The long roster of republican structures should put it beyond dispute that the leading features of the Florentine physiognomy even as late as the present day are pre-Medicean. And being pre-Medicean they are also pre-Renaissance. But that does not mean that when the turn of the Medici and the Renaissance came—and the cue word for their historical appearance fell at the same moment of time—they did not add important touches to the town's outstanding features. Above all, since the Renaissance was nothing other than the revival of learning transferred to the field of the arts, it deposited numerous evidences in the town of its new and very different esthetic orientation. The champion of the new outlook in the realm of architecture was Filippo Brunelleschi, and the substance of his artistic message was the return to the classical principles of construction, more particularly to the column-and-lintel or column-and-arch characteristic of the ancient temple. Cosimo, as it happened, first came to the front politically while the new movement was engaged in getting a foothold; and since he promptly extended his patronage to Brunelleschi, he and the new architecture made their debut simultaneously on the Florentine scene. But that cannot and must not be interpreted as meaning that the architect in any even remote way owed his esthetic inspiration to the merchant.

For our statement on pre-Medicean sculpture we shall abandon the chronological for the more revealing evolutionary approach. The beginnings of sculpture within the boundaries of Tuscany must be sought in Pisa. Thence, after some decades, the practice of the art spread upstream to Florence. Consequently, the first Florentine sculptor of note was a Pisan native, as is clearly revealed by his name, Andrea Pisano. To him goes the honor of having called a native Florentine sculpture to life by fashioning between 1330 and 1336 the first or southern bronze doors of the baptistery of San Giovanni. Within a lively frame of foliage and figures in the round we are confronted with twenty scenes from the life of St. John fashioned with such economy of means and rhythm of design that their author was at once accepted as the inspired leader in his field.

Andrea had been the pupil back in Pisa of Giovanni Pisano (d. 1328) whose fame rests on his having impressed a definitely Gothic pattern on his work. While Andrea, an independent spirit, departed notably from his master's style, such was Giovanni's authority in his day that it was he, and not Andrea, who set the sculptural fashion for the remainder of the fourteenth century throughout not only Tuscany but most of Italy as well. Consequently, the sculptors who worked in Florence after Andrea's time turned out Gothically inspired pieces, conventional, pedestrian stuff in the main, save for the single shrine of our Lady in Or San Michele. This is the work of Andrea Orcagna (d. 1368), who labored at it for so many decades and with such unremitting devotion that his shrine stands out as one of the most amazing combinations of delicate, jewel-like inlay and of sculpture in the round and in relief within the whole range of Italian art.

The Gothic utterance was becoming feebler and feebler when it was abandoned altogether in favor of a new plastic speech which, in final analysis, exactly as in the case of architecture, had its origin in the revival of learning. It was this stirring intellectual movement that swung the attention of the new generation of sculptors to the sculpture of antiquity, of which individual specimens, or fragments of specimens, might be encountered all over Italy but considerable quantities only at Rome. Early in the fifteenth century a young Florentine resolved to give himself the better schooling in the manner of the ancients that Rome alone afforded and betook himself thither to make sketches from such originals as had not yet completely disappeared under the heaped debris of the past. The young man was Donatello and fortunately he was not content to be a mere copyist and imitator. Instinctively sensing that ancient sculpture owed its vitality to its closeness to life, he balanced his devotion to antiquity with a devotion to nature and by the inspiration he drew from both these sources enabled Florentine sculpture to enter on a new phase.

However, Donatello was not a lonely, isolated figure. There, for instance, was Lorenzo Ghiberti, who played a creative role quite on a level with his own. Between them they breathed a new spirit into sculpture well in advance of Cosimo de' Medici's appearance on the scene. All that remained for Cosimo to do was to provide a well-launched movement with the stimulus of his generous patronage.

On turning next to painting, we take up the art which was peculiarly suited to the genius of the Florentines and in which their production proved so significant that it has to an extraordinary extent determined the whole later course of European expression in this art. The beginnings of Florentine practice point to Byzantine models which, at first contentedly copied, were gradually modified under independent inspiration. The first native painter of note was Cimabue. He was completely overshadowed by his pupil, Giotto, who, when he died in 1337, left behind a body of work which not only blazed the path for whoever came after him in Florence but which in addition placed him in the select group of the great masters through the ages.

Giotto practiced both fresco and panel panting, two methods which he took over from his predecessors. His fresco work proved incomparably more important than the much more rarely practiced panel painting. Its technique, reduced to its simplest terms, consisted in applying color to fresh plaster, and admirably lent itself to covering the spacious interior walls of churches with scenes from the lives of the Savior, the Virgin Mary, and the saints. It was by this method that Giotto created an unrivaled pictorial version of the moving stories of the Christian faith. His dominating means of expression was the human figure, which he endowed with such dignity and animated with such dramatic power that the spectator was able at a glance to capture both the substance and the significance of the pictured scene.

So great was the authority wielded in his day by Giotto that literally scores of disciples obediently and blindly followed in his footsteps. Their work may still be seen in churches scattered over Italy but, owing to the flaking of the ancient plaster, it is slowly disappearing and will in all probability ultimately completely vanish. This will be no artistic loss as regards the mass of their paintings, for Giotto's followers, as has been the case with all worshipers of success through the centuries, contented themselves with imitation of the master and failed to endow their pictures with the individual life alone capable of giving them enduring value. With decline continuing through several generations painting at last glowed with so feeble a spark that it might have perished, had it not experienced a rebirth due to the same agency that effected the rebirth of the equally decadent Gothic sculpture. It need hardly be expressly said that this agency was the revival of learning and antiquity.

We saw in the case of sculpture that the return to antiquity prompted also a return to nature. The identical double influence of nature and antiquity made itself felt also among the painters with the result that presently a young genius, Masaccio by name, brought them to the richest conceivable expression in his work. He did not fail, however, to make a return also to Giotto and to re-absorb Giotto's vital treatment of the human figure. Masaccio died in 1428 at the early age of twenty-seven and left behind him in Florence hardly anything more than a single fresco series in the Carmine church on the left bank of the

Arno. But this lone series sufficed for him to play the same renewal role among the painters that Ghiberti and Donatello
played among the sculptors and Brunelleschi among the architects. With them the brilliant phase of native art, named from
its century the *quattrocento* phase, was started on its triumphant way. Of this movement Cosimo de' Medici made himself
the liberal sponsor but had of course nothing to do with endowing it with its inner significance and flaming vigor.

IV

THE RISE OF COSIMO

EVERY reader of Dante will recall with what swelling pride he proclaimed that his was among the most ancient families of Florence. He made the boast indirectly through the mouth of his ancestor, Cacciaguida, encountered in paradise, goal and reward of the upright, but it loses none of its personal fervor on that account. At the same time the scornful aristocrat took occasion to vent his spite on the stinking peasants who for a hundred years preceding his time had been pouring into Florence from such neighboring villages as Campi, Certaldo, and Fighine, and who by their unwelcome invasion had quintupled the population since Cacciaguida's day.

Among these despised invaders were the ancestors of the family destined after many generations to rise to the headship of the city. It was around the year 1200 that first one and then another individual bearing the Medici name abandoned his farm in the mountainous Mugello region north of Florence to seek his fortune in the rapidly expanding commune. Convincing evidence of the family's Mugello origin is furnished by the unbroken connection maintained with it through ownership of property at Cafaggiolo in the Mugello throughout the period of their grandeur.

The newcomers must have succeeded in taking excellent advantage of the opportunities offered by prospering Florence, for when, in the year 1282, the republican government, called the government of the priors, was formed, members of the family were already found enrolled among the greater guilds, that is to say, among the leading merchants of the town. As early as 1291 a certain Ardingo de' Medici is named as prior and in 1296 this same Ardingo served as gonfalonier. In the following, the fourteenth, century a constantly increasing number of members of the clan are mentioned in the documents in the capacity either of merchants and guild members or of priors. Without question the family was on the upgrade, was steadily rising in the world. However, no public event of particular significance occurred in association with its name until we come to Salvestro de' Medici.

With Salvestro the family was for the first time definitely lifted into general view. As already related in an earlier chapter, while serving as gonfalonier, in June, 1378, he instigated a successful coup against a group of high-born political manipulators, thereby winning standing and reputation as an enemy of the oligarchic monopolizers of power and, consequently, as a friend of the people. From Salvestro's time the humbler Florentines, especially the members of the lesser guilds, were firmly persuaded that the Medici were the one major guild clan which could be counted on to champion their cause. However, a generation passed before another Medici succeeded in making his name a household word in the town. He was Giovanni di Bicci, that is, Giovanni, son of Bicci, and in a merchant commonwealth like Florence he was bound to kindle discussion, since he had by his business genius made himself lord of one of the great fortunes of the day. As soon as this fact had become well established the common people, viewing him with the Medici bias they had nursed since Salvestro's time, confidently expected him to play his part as their advocate.

It was a role which Giovanni never assumed, possibly because he was not ambitious politically, more probably because he was completely absorbed in business. The period was that of the Albizzi oligarchy, which had entered on possession of power in 1382. Born in 1360 in comparative poverty, Giovanni did not belong to the ruling merchant clique and was looked down on by the possessors of older wealth as a *novus homo,* an upstart. Their scorn—or was it envy?—did not, however, keep them from treating him with a certain consideration, for the Albizzi rule, especially so long as its founder, Maso degli Albizzi, lived, bore a moderate character and took the stand that it was better to conciliate than to beat down and trample possible rivals. Consequently, Giovanni was repeatedly elected to the priorate and once at least, in 1421, was promoted to the highest office in the state, the gonfalonierat. When, at a later time, an irreconcilable feud broke out between the sons respectively of Maso and Giovanni, it was not unnaturally, but with little justification in point of fact, projected backward on their fathers. We are almost certainly right in thinking of the politically unambitious Giovanni as contentedly pushing the interests of his merchant company, which after the manner of these organizations from the time of their origin represented a combination of trade and banking. Giovanni seems to have emphasized banking more than merchandising and by his energy piled up a fortune that put him in the top flight of local capitalists.

How readily legend can displace fact is well illustrated by the last important event in which Giovanni figured. A war conducted with Milan between 1422 and 1428 had exhausted the Florentine treasury before it could be brought to an end, thereby obliging the government to seek fresh sources of revenue. Prolonged discussion in the councils ended with their resorting for the first time in the town's history to an income tax. It received the name of the *catasto* from the register of the citizens' possessions on which the tax was based. The catasto was adopted in 1427 at a time when the Albizzi rule was as yet unchallenged and unimpaired. When, a hundred years later, Machiavelli in his *History of Florence* reached the catasto he was greatly puzzled, since he had observed that oligarchies invariably favored indirect over direct taxes and that the Florentine oligarchy had thus far behaved exactly as expected. Given much more to political reflection than to time-robbing historical research, Machiavelli offered as explanation of the surprising phenomenon of 1427 that Giovanni di Bicci, backed by a clamorous public opinion, had forced the oligarchy against their will and interest to adopt the new tax. So plausible was the contention that it was generally accepted and still figures in the indestructible Florentine legend—this, in spite of the fact that a nineteenth century investigator, who, contrary to Machiavelli's indolent practice, was moved to consult the actual council debates, discovered that Giovanni had been either openly hostile or feebly luke-warm to the catasto proposal, and that it had been carried by the oligarchs themselves under the leadership of Rinaldo degli Albizzi and Niccolò da Uzzano.[1]

Giovanni di Bicci died in February, 1429, not much more than a year after the adoption of the revolutionary income tax. All the available facts support the view that, although there had been differences of opinion between him and the oligarchs, they had never been carried to an open breach. That development did not come until Giovanni had been succeeded by his son, Cosimo, and even then it came only after Rinaldo degli Albizzi, the unofficial ruler of the city, had launched a war against neighboring Lucca—and lost it.

Ever since Florence had embarked on the policy of uniting Tuscany under its rule it had repeatedly but invariably without success engaged in a war of conquest against Lucca. With the grinding Milanese war ended in 1428, it might have been thought

[1] The scholar's name is P. Berti. See "Nuovi Documenti intorno al Catasto Fiorentino," *Giornale Storico degli Archivi Toscani*, Vol. IV, pp. 32-62.

that a long period of rest and recuperation was in order. That was not the opinion of Rinaldo degli Albizzi, now pretty much in exclusive control of the oligarchic junta. He knew he could count on the fervent support of the Florentine masses, since it had always been easy to fan their passions to flame against the stubborn little republic to their west. His design was aided by the circumstance that Lucca seemed at the moment to be so completely isolated politically that it would go down in defeat before a helper could arrive on the scene. Accordingly, in 1429 Rinaldo launched an attack which, in spite of its wantonness, enjoyed the frenzied support of the entire Florentine population. Even Cosimo, the new head of the as yet loosely cohering Medici faction, gave it his blessing and, in sign of his approval, accepted service on the board of war, the *Dieci* (the Ten).

Rinaldo's rosy expectations turned out to be a bundle of bad guesses. The Lucchese got prompt and abundant help from their neighbors, unanimously averse to having Florence add another gem to its already jewel-studded crown; the mercenary armies engaged by the Arno city made their usual bad showing; and the headlong Rinaldo, who had personally taken the field, gravely bungled the successive campaigns with his ill-considered measures. The calamitous struggle was spun out for four years, at the end of which the prospect of capturing Lucca had grown so dim that Rinaldo was glad to wash his hands of the whole evil mess by making peace (May 10, 1433).

When the Florentines enthusiastically backed Rinaldo's war against Lucca, they had done so in the persuasion usual among war-makers that success was as good as assured. On victory eluding them, again like war-makers before and since, instead of beating their breasts in repentance, they heaped the blame on their unhappy leader. The bitter criticism shook Rinaldo's political grip and made him extremely restive and jittery. Not content with talk, his emboldened critics looked about for someone with whom they might hope to replace him and found their man in Rinaldo's most conspicuous rival, Cosimo de' Medici.

While Cosimo, too, had supported the war, he was not prepared to shoulder the blame for Rinaldo's blundering measures, and by an occasional open word, supplemented by an effective whispering campaign, encouraged the spreading opposition to the leading oligarch. Being, however, an extremely cautious soul by nature, in the summer following the peace with Lucca he withdrew from the overheated Florentine scene to his distant farm in the quiet Mugello hills. Should there be an explosion, as was not unlikely, Cosimo preferred not to be around when it occurred.

Rinaldo, who was Cosimo's direct temperamental opposite, stayed on at Florence and curbed his habitual impatience as long as he could. Only when, on September 1, a group of priors with a gonfalonier at their head took office who in their majority were of his party and ready to co-operate with him, did he decide on action. Accordingly, an order was dispatched to Cosimo at his villa in the mountains to appear before the government and when, on September 7, he presented himself in their chamber, he was promptly arrested and locked up in a small cell high up in the soaring tower of the palace of the priors. From there through a narrow slit that served as a window he could, if he wished, watch the happenings on the spacious piazza below.

What, two days after his arrest, unfolded before Cosimo's eyes was a constitutional comedy of darkest import for himself. At this point we must halt our narrative to insert an explanation. The government of the priors had by now been in operation for about one hundred and fifty years, but not without having passed through a number of the gravest crises. On the Albizzi oligarchy seizing power it had developed a plan for overcoming a peril threatening its rule by means of an instrument that reached back to the earliest history of the commune. That instrument was the parliament of the people conceived as the final source of political power. However, since the Ordinances of Justice of 1293, which constituted the legal foundation of the priorate, took no account of the parliament, it no longer had any standing in law. This did not prevent the Albizzi oligarchs from appropriating and adapting it to their use. Whenever, during their domination, an opposition group appeared which threatened to become dangerous or whenever a minority in their own ranks fell out of step, the leading oligarchs had called a parliament to request leave for the appointment of a committee with power (*balìa*) to "reform" the government. Through the device of letting only known partisans of the faction in control pass through the several narrow entrances to the piazza, the assembled parliament was a strictly partisan affair and voted the proposed committee by acclamation. Thereupon the committee, usually called balìa from the special power wherewith it was endowed, in one way or another, but most commonly by exile (*confino*), outlawed the citizens whom the ruling oligarchs were pleased to regard as disturbers of the peace. Then, its work done, the balìa retired from the scene and the regular government again took over.

Undebatably the parliament, kept in reserve as an institution for the single purpose of eliminating individuals or groups actually or prospectively dangerous to the ruling clique, was, constitutionally considered, a hoax and a sham. But it conferred an undeniable social benefit in that it secured a desirable continuity of government and avoided the evils of riot and bloodshed regularly attendant on revolution. If we compare Florentine internal history with the internal history of such neighboring communes as Pistoia, Pisa, and Siena, we shall find that it was marked by far fewer convulsions and that the improved domestic record is plainly owing to the relative permanence of government achieved by the crooked device of the parliament. In support of the view that it served as an indispensable prop of the ruling group we may note by anticipation that, when the Medici succeeded the Albizzi as rulers of the city, they depended on the identical trick of the parliament for beating down a rising opposition and exhibited the same lack of scruple in its use as their predecessors.

Since Cosimo was a citizen born and educated in Florence, he could not for even a moment have been in doubt as to the meaning of the spectacle which, on September 9, unfolded under his eyes. The pouring of the people into the piazza must have had for him a purpose as clear as the sun overhead: they had been called together to validate a balìa to determine his fate. The usual all-powerful committee, which on this occasion was a sizable affair of two hundred members, continued in debate for many days and voiced a great variety of opinions. At last, on September 29, it settled on a verdict, which had become more or less customary through its adoption on similar occasions, and condemned Cosimo, his brother Lorenzo, and a number of outstanding Medicean partisans to exile in various specifically designated towns of Italy. A few days later the victims were taken under guard to the frontier and Cosimo and Lorenzo made their way to Venice, their appointed residence. The Venetians, unimpressed by the bogus charges against Cosimo, honored him on his arrival with a reception more befitting a king on his travels than a discredited and uprooted commoner.

At a later time Cosimo wrote an account of his arrest and imprisonment, entitled *Ricordi,* which is an interesting confession for both what it says and what it does not say.[1] It is an unadorned statement of fact ruffled with not as much as a passing flicker of emotion. And while it truthfully lists the main happenings, it throws no light on a number of interesting surmises connected with the arrest and its solution which have sufficient foundation in fact to merit inclusion in our story. One surmise, in its origin no more than a generally current rumor, ran to the effect that the imprisoned Cosimo was so convinced that his enemies planned to remove him by poison that he refused to eat until, to reassure him, his jailer volunteered to share his meals. Another surmise dealt with the verdict which sent him into exile rather than, as was widely expected, to his death. The

---

[1] William Roscoe, *The Life of Lorenzo de' Medici,* 10th ed. 2 vols. Bell and Sons, London, 1895. The *Ricordi* will be found in the Appendix.

milder sentence was attributed to a change of opinion on the part of the hostile gonfalonier, whom Cosimo was declared to have reached with a handsome bribe. Even in case it could be shown that these conjectures are completely lacking in substance, they would still deserve to be recorded because they bring home something of the suspicion, intrigue, and devious maneuvers that in large part made up the political background of Florence not only at this but at every period of its history.

In spite of Rinaldo's having got rid of his Medici enemy, his position after Cosimo's departure was hardly less insecure than before. Continuing to hold him responsible for the recent Lucchese catastrophe, his fellow citizens found less and less reason for putting up with his native arrogance. While he for his part resented their attitude, there was nothing he could effectually do to change it. Therefore, every time the election came round for a new signory—the common designation for the executive of priors and gonfalonier—he was stretched as on tenterhooks from fear that an enemy majority would leap from the ballot box. Since each signory lasted only two months, even a favorable election gave him no better than a reprieve. Fortunately for him the next five elections went his way. But the sixth was a disaster. On September 1, 1434, a pro-Medicean government took office and exactly a year after the condemnation of the Medicean faction undertook to undo its predecessor's work.

Rinaldo flew into a rage over this turn in his fortunes, but even in a rage displayed the mettle of a man of action. Since the loss of the signory was the certain warrant of his early overthrow, he resolved to seize the palace by force and drive out his enemies. When to this end he gathered his armed partisans about him, the signory collected a force of its own for its defense and the outbreak of civil war hung by a thread. It did not break out because of an understandable reluctance of both parties to draw the sword supplemented by the intervention of a mediator.

The mediator was none other than the head of Christendom,

Pope Eugene IV. He had recently been driven from Rome by a local rebellion and at the invitation of the Florentines had sought refuge in their city. He had made the great Dominican monastery of Santa Maria Novella his headquarters and, on hearing of the threatening civil war, offered, as befitted his high office, to mediate between the opposed factions. At Eugene's request Rinaldo, who was an obedient son of the church, went to see him in his quarters at San Domenico and inevitably became entangled in long-spun-out negotiations. On this sign of irresolution his none too devoted followers dispersed and his cause was lost. Thereupon the signory no longer hesitated. Resorting to the familiar trick of a parliament, it had a balìa appointed with power to see the government through the crisis. Its first act was to cancel the decree of exile against Cosimo, his brother, and his closest supporters and to invite them to return to the city with all possible dispatch. It then completed the "reform" for which it was created by punishing Rinaldo and his most compromised adherents with the same sentence of exile which its predecessor had inflicted on its own adversaries.

Speeding home from Venice, Cosimo, as with restrained exultation he notes in his *Ricordi,* crossed the Florentine border on his way back on the precise day, that is, October 5, on which he had crossed it on his way out in the previous year of 1433. He was given a wild welcome by his fellow townsmen and in association with his Medicean junta of henchmen took over the control of the city which he then never again relinquished. Aside from the sentences of exile already passed against his leading opponents, there were no irregularities save a brief spasm of violence which Cosimo found it necessary to concede to the intemperate element among his followers before they would let him quietly settle down to his work. It is more than likely, it is as good as certain that, had Cosimo been in sole command, which he was not, he would have dispensed with punishments inspired exclusively by a spirit of revenge; for, in addition to his addiction to moderate courses, which is the true mark of a statesman, he possessed a genuinely humane disposition. After one of his rare assumptions of the highest office in the state, the gonfalonierat, he noted in his *Ricordi* with evident inner satisfaction that during his incumbency "no one was exiled or subjected to ill treatment."

Under these exceptionally felicitous auspices Cosimo embarked on the rule of his native city.

Baptistery of St. John

Brogi

Palace of the Podestà, later called Bargello

Palace of the Signory, now called Palazzo Vecchio

Cathedral of Santa Maria del Fiore and Giotto's Campanile

Brogi

Interior of San Lorenzo (BRUNELLESCHI)

Cloister of San Marco Monastery (MICHELOZZO)

Courtyard of Medici Palace (MICHELOZZO)

Brogi

Medici Palace (MICHELOZZO)

Brogi

Brogi

DONATELLO. King David, popularly known as the Pumpkin Head.

Brogi

GHIBERTI. Main Baptistery Gate.

Brogi

VERROCCHIO. David.

FRA ANGELICO. Coronation of the Virgin.

MASACCIO. The Holy Trinity with the Virgin, St. John, and Donors. Fresco. Santa Maria Novella.

Brogi

ZZOLI. From *Procession of the Kings*. Fresco. Chapel of the Medici Palace.

BOTTICELLI. Birth of Venus.

Brogi

MICHELANGELO. New Sacristy of San Lorenzo showing the monument to Giuliano de' Medici.

Giovanni
di Bicci
de' Medici

Cosimo
de' Medici

Lorenzo the
Magnificent.
Death Mask.

Piero
di Lorenzo
de' Medici
(VERROCCHIO)

Pope Leo X
(RAPHAEL)

Brogi

CLEMENS. VII. PONT. MAX. IVLIANI MED. F.

Pope
Clement VII

Alinari

V

THE RULE OF COSIMO

THE government of Florence, which Cosimo took over in 1434, remained in his hands until his death thirty years later. Since it constitutes an outstanding chapter of Florentine political and cultural history, it calls for a close scrutiny, which cannot be better inaugurated than by having a look at its author on his assumption of power. When, on his death, his work had been done and the record was closed, we shall return to him for a final appraisal.

Cosimo was born in the year 1389 and therefore stood on the summit of existence when he became the unofficial ruler of his city. In his youth at school he had been nourished on the medieval curriculum of Latin, logic, and arithmetic, modified to a not unimportant extent by the intrusion of the recently revived classical studies. Consequently, he was not just following a fashionable trend when in his mature years he became the friend and patron of the promoters of these studies. However, let it be noted at once and never forgotten that the influences that mainly shaped his mind were business and politics. These were the twin elements in which the Florentine merchant class had steeped itself ever since the rise of the commune. Certainly his father, Giovanni di Bicci, had been immersed in them with the notable individual quirk that he set a preferred value on business. For evidence of his settled merchant character we do not have to go further than to the portrait the sixteenth century painter, Bronzino, copied from an earlier painting executed by a contemporary of Giovanni's. Than the original behind this portrait it is hard to imagine anyone more rooted in the practical concerns of life, although it may be conceded that a troubled kindliness about the eyes softens the impression of a too exclusive devotion to his business ledger.

Such a father would not fail to apprentice both his sons, for, besides Cosimo, there was a younger son, Lorenzo by name, to his expanding banking business and, as they advanced in years, to dispatch them on missions to its multiplying branches. He would also urge them to accept the honors of public office when they came their way, for we must not forget that, although Giovanni was not a member of the ruling Albizzi faction, he had no insuperable quarrel with it either and repeatedly was promoted to the highest posts in the republic. The assertion holds also for Cosimo, who, certainly not without Albizzi consent, served more than once as prior and, during both the Milanese war of the twenties and the Lucchese war of the thirties that promptly followed, was a member of the powerful war committee, the Dieci.

While the replacement of the Albizzi by the Medici was an outstanding domestic event, it was far from constituting the sharp break in the Florentine political tradition as which it was afterward presented. Too exclusively under the impression of the relative permanence of the Medicean rule, later historians tended to divide the city's history into two segments separated by an unbridgeable chasm. No such division is justified on the basis of political changes introduced in 1434. Cosimo took over the system of the Albizzi, as the Albizzi had taken over that of their predecessors, the Black Guelphs, with no more than a single change. But that change was crucial and largely accounts for the tight and unshaken rule which Cosimo achieved. To grasp its full significance we shall have to turn back to an earlier page of Florentine history.

The Ordinances of Justice of 1293 provided for the election of the priors and gonfalonier—the signory—in a fair and orderly way. Since this was precisely what the merchant clique aspiring to control did not want, the elections were from the start unscrupulously manipulated in the merchant interest. Thereupon, after a generation, in 1328 to be exact, a method of election was adopted which was supposed to put an end to the continued and apparently ineradicable underhand practices of the group in power. Honest in outward appearance, it gave additional satisfaction by flattering the passion for equality among the members of the guilds, to whom, we must never forget, the privilege of holding political office exclusively pertained. The new system consisted in assembling in a heap the names of all the guildsmen who survived what was called the *scrutinio*, that is, the scrutiny or examination of the guild lists in regard to the political reliability of each individual member. The names of the eligibles were then deposited in leather bags or purses called *borse*. The borse were kept under lock and key until the day fixed for the bimestrial election, when they were brought out and the new signory picked, as it were, out of a grab-bag of names. The total procedure received the designation of "election by lot" and, in witness of the inborn and incurable irrationality of man, was extolled by its promoters, the guildsmen, as the last word in political wisdom.

Of course it did not work. The junta in power at once resumed the secret manipulations which, long customary, now became indispensable if the government, constitutionally deprived of continuity, was to enjoy even a small measure of effectiveness. It will at once appear that all that was henceforth necessary in order to control the offices was to control the borse. When the Albizzi oligarchs seized the power, they elaborated a procedure

which secured them the relatively long continuance of their
rule. Whenever the legally required drawings by lot produced a
larger percentage of opponents of their regime than they considered safe, they would call a parliament and have a committee
(or balìa) appointed to effect a "reform." This signified nothing
other than a fresh review (or scrutiny) by which the names of
all known opponents of the group in power were kept out of
the borse—and the game was won! There was just one hitch. A
change of opinion might come over the men whose names had
gone into the purses, and before the purses could be again "reformed," a hostile signory might have resulted from an early
subsequent drawing by lot. This was the very mischance that
had caused the downfall of Rinaldo degli Albizzi. On September 1, 1434, he and his gang were swept off the boards by a
pro-Medicean signory duly picked from the borse.

It was the defect in the Albizzi system of control that Cosimo
resolved to correct, and the correction, as already indicated,
largely explains his more secure tenure. But to represent it as
the earliest departure from free to controlled elections is of
course legendary, anti-Medicean nonsense. What Cosimo did was
simplicity itself: he retained the scrutiny and borse but replaced
the drawings by lot of the members of the signory with their
designation by a committee of ten electors called *accoppiatori*.
He had this committee given power for five years and, on the
expiration of its term, had its power renewed for another five-
year period. The ten electors were strict Medicean partisans,
and since they picked the officials out of the borse by hand (*a
mano,* as the local gibe ran), the signory was so unwaveringly
Medicean that it was beyond the danger of overthrow save by
a general uprising.

In the operation of his government Cosimo observed an intelligent reserve, which cannot be sufficiently praised in view
of the complicated character of his control. As the head of
an oligarchic faction, he could not afford to be too much in
the public eye, since his associates inclined to regard themselves

as his equals and would have deeply resented a too open and sweeping assumption of power on his part. Only three times, in 1435, in 1439, and in 1445, did he let himself be promoted to the high office of gonfalonier, that is, during a rule of thirty years he was the visible head of the state for a total of six months! You also looked for him in vain among the accoppia tori, the ten electors, for he allocated this powerful office exclusively to his fellow oligarchs. The only employment through which he emerged as a public servant and to which he let himself be regularly re-elected was membership on the board of the National Debt, called the *Monte*. This placed him at the very center of the Florentine finances and was so important for the smooth running of the government that he did not mind letting it be generally known that he was putting his admired capacity as a banker at the service of the commonwealth.

When we turn from domestic to foreign affairs we come upon the really decisive explanation of why it was that the system of election by lot would not work. Florence had become involved in a power struggle with four other Italian states, with Venice, Milan, Naples, and the papacy, that required a much more alert and uninterrupted attention than was possible to a haphazard executive with the life of a meager two months. The demand of political logic was therefore to surrender the bimestrial turnover; but in case this could not be effected in the face of a perverted public opinion, the alternative was for an invisible power superior to the signory to take over the foreign department. It was the necessity of a firm and at the same time elastic policy in regard to the neighbors of Florence which in last analysis explains the gravest irregularities of the several pre-Medicean regimes and which may be said to have become imperative from the moment the Arno republic aspired to rank as an Italian power. Cosimo's insight on this head is another reason for paying ready tribute to his political intelligence. So undebatably important did he consider the department of foreign affairs to be that there was in his view no escape from taking it over as his special domain. But here again, owing to the sleepless jealousy of his party associates and to that of the whole Florentine population as well, he had to tread warily. While leaving the exchange of official correspondence to the priors in their palace, he had to spin a supplementary diplomatic web behind the backs of the priors from his private residence. The conduct of foreign affairs from two offices, one public, the other private, required an inexhaustible treasure of tact on Cosimo's part and, even so, would have broken down, had it not been for the immense, imponderable prestige he had succeeded in assembling, alike at home and abroad, by reason of his effective handling of both his bank and the government.

After this general statement on method let us turn to the events that make up the story of Cosimo's rule and let us pay our respects not only to those of a strictly political nature but also to those which, belonging to the wider social realm, have the merit of revealing something of the tang and color of contemporary life. As we have noted, the pope, Eugene IV, on being driven from Rome had, during the last months of the Albizzi regime, taken residence in Florence. He found it convenient to stay on for almost a decade, during which period the Arno city figured in effect as the capital of Christendom and shone forth with a redoubled splendor. A man as resourceful as Cosimo was sure to make this exceptional situation in one way or another redound to the advantage of his town, and at least two such occasions are highlighted in the record.

As the leading item of local conversation at the time of Cosimo's advent to power there figured the completion of architect Brunelleschi's vast cupola of the cathedral of Santa Maria del Fiore. The edifice could now at last be consecrated, and with the head of the church available as the main actor of the piece, Cosimo resolved to stage a spectacle, the talk of which would make the round of Christendom. Accordingly, the consecration was set for March 25, 1436, which was the Feast of the Annunciation and which by the very individual calendar of the Florentines was reckoned also as the first day of the New Year. As the pope resided at the Dominican monastery of Santa Maria Novella, a raised board walk was constructed leading from there to the cathedral. With its canopy and sides made festive with banners and garlands it drew, when the appointed day arrived, the entire population and held it breathless with wonder as there passed over the carpeted walk the tiara-crowned pope in white, attended by seven cardinals in flaming red, thirty-seven empurpled bishops and archbishops, and in the wake of this ecclesiastical magnificence the more soberly but still resplendently costumed civil government of the priors and gonfalonier. The gorgeous train came to a halt at the altar erected under the soaring dome, where the act of dedication concluded the day's impressive drama. Their participation from the side-lines in an engrossing spectacle may have been reckoned by the humble woolen workers, over whose bent backs the colorful procession of the world's elect may figuratively be said to have marched, as payment on account of their heaped wage arrears.

Three years later, in 1439, an even greater splendor radiated from Florence, of which Pope Eugene was again the point of origin. Negotiations he had been conducting with dignitaries of the estranged Greek Orthodox church at Constantinople had persuaded him that the rift between the two Christian churches, which had opened six hundred years before, could be closed by discussions conducted in a General Council. He had no reason to think, at least no plausible reason, that the stubborn division of opinion on points of doctrine, which had caused the schism, had abated after six centuries, but he was aware that a political situation had developed at Constantinople which might have the effect of bringing the Greeks to terms. That situation had been precipitated by the Ottoman Turks. Having successfully encroached on the Greek empire for the previous hundred years, they were now drawing their lines closer and closer around the apparently doomed capital in preparation for the final leap. With no human help in sight save from the Latin west, the

Greek emperor, John Paleologus, resolved to make the submission to the pope without which by way of preliminary no help would be forthcoming from the Catholic world. He persuaded the patriarch, as the head of the Greek church was called, to accept the pope's invitation to the General Council and, attended by the patriarch and other leading personages of the eastern church, set out on the arduous journey to the distant city on the Arno.

It was the Turk dagger at the Greek throat and not the dialectical skill of its erudite theologians that won the case for the Latin church. Yielding ground inch by inch, the Greek fathers at last accepted a sufficient number of doctrinal definitions proposed by their Latin opposites to create an appearance of agreement; and on July 5, 1439, in a final ceremonial session held in the cathedral of Santa Maria del Fiore the lost unity of Christianity was declared to have been providentially restored. Whoever is familiar with this ancient edifice will recall that on one of the huge piers that support Brunelleschi's soaring dome appears an inscription immortalizing the event. In trumpet tones it booms forth the good news that the two churches had accommodated their ancient differences and re-established a united Christian world.

Hardly had the Florentine stone-cutters incised the commemorative statement when the word reached the west that the Greeks on reaching home had been obliged by an aroused public opinion to repudiate the union. This promptly flattened out the General Council to a historical hoax, which continues to this day to touch off amused laughter by the reflection that the five hundred years that have elapsed since the Florentine fiasco have not sufficed to bring about the union proclaimed as an accomplished fact by the lapidary boast. Except for the negligible matter of the lively entertainment afforded the Florentine population by the coming and going through many months of so many of the world's great dignitaries, the Council of 1439 might be written off as a total loss, were it not for a benefit that ultimately accrued from a literary project sponsored on the occasion of the Council by Cosimo de' Medici.

Quite the most distinguished of the Greek visitors was a reverent, silver-bearded septuagenarian, George Gemistus Plethon, a theologian of course but also and primarily a philosopher. He was in fact a passionate exponent of the philosophy of Plato, whom the exclusive vogue of his pupil, Aristotle, during the Middle Ages had consigned to all but complete oblivion. True, the humanists had recently brought Plato again to the notice of the western peoples; but not until Plethon formally expounded him at Florence before a hushed assembly of Italian scholars did he again become a living intellectual force. Cosimo, too, fell under the spell cast by the eloquent and imposing Plethon, and would have liked to retain him in Florence in order to found with his help an academy for Platonic studies. But the Greek's heart was set on home and Cosimo was obliged regretfully to abandon his plan. But not for good. Some years later he revived it on discovering, as will be disclosed in the succeeding chapter, in young Marsilio Ficino the energy and genius necessary to create the center of Platonic learning which Cosimo had never ceased to cherish as a desirable project.

When Rinaldo degli Albizzi and his supporters were driven from the city, it was certain that they would make every effort to come back. Nor in their frenzied search for helpers would they hesitate to knock at the door of their country's enemies. The foremost enemy of Florence at this time was, as we learned in the previous chapter, Filippo Maria, the Visconti duke of Milan, and the enmity between him and the Arno republic arose from his persistent desire to extend his power southward into Tuscany and the Romagna, the northernmost province of the States of the Church. Since the interests of the Florentine state obliged its government to block this advance, there was perpetual friction between the two powers which had already repeatedly resulted in war.

It was this situation which induced Rinaldo to seek support from Milan, to which its duke hesitated for a long time to accede with anything better than half and quarter measures. Not till the year 1440 did he order Piccinino, one of the several condottieri he was in the habit of employing, to lead an army against the Arno city with the plan of restoring Rinaldo to his former control. Since Florence, like every other Italian state, conducted its wars with mercenary troops freshly engaged for each fresh occasion, it was unprepared to meet the sudden attack, and the Milanese army, with the Florentine exiles leading the way, pushed across the Apennines and arrived on the heights of Fiesole above Florence without encountering resistance. Duke Filippo Maria had been confidently assured by the exiles that his army would have but to appear before Florence for the citizens to rise in revolution against the tyrant Cosimo and open the gates to Rinaldo as to a savior. When not a mouse stirred in the town, Piccinino recognized that he had been served the delusions usual among exiles from the beginning of time and, lacking the means to conduct the siege of so large a city, marched off to the Casentino in the upper Arno in search of supplies. He was followed thither by the Florentine army, as soon as one could be brought together, and, on June 29, 1440, a battle took place at Anghiari which ended in a Milanese rout. Piccinino was obliged to abandon Tuscany and with him went the dejected Florentine exiles. When Rinaldo, high-spirited to the end, died two years later, the old oligarchy may be said to have been laid with him into the grave. In any case the Medicean rule was never again challenged from that quarter.

The sweeping victory brought a number of advantages which considerably strengthened Cosimo's hold on the city. In the mountainous Casentino the ancient feudal lords had maintained themselves longer than in the fertile lowlands of Tuscany but nonetheless had latterly been brought progressively to heel. The outstanding exception was the greatest lord of them all, the count of Poppi, although the count was not an unqualified exception since he owed his continued existence to his at least formal acceptance of the republic's supremacy. In an attack of sublunary madness the reigning count joined Piccinino on his invasion of the Casentino and on Piccinino's defeat was driven from his lands and the lands themselves incorporated in the Florentine state. The castle of Poppi, which devouring time has fortunately spared, still overwhelms every sensitive visitor with its feudal grandeur. If the visitor happens also to be history-minded, he will not fail to be touched with the melancholy that envelops every completed human destiny as he recalls that the counts of Poppi were the last offshoot of the Guidi, a family which, back in the twelfth and thirteenth centuries, was said to command as many castles as there were days in the year and for whose support even emperors did not feel too exalted to sue.

The standing quarrel between Florence and Duke Filippo Maria continued after, as before, the Piccinino campaign. As long as the restless ruler of Milan refused to surrender his territorial ambitions the peace that followed a war was never anything better than a truce. If in the years under review he made no headway worth mentioning, it was because his two powerful neighbors, Florence and Venice, maintained an alliance pledged to resist every new territorial encroachment he might be pleased to undertake.

Slowly, however, another factor was injected into the situation which at last fundamentally altered it. That factor was the Milanese succession crisis which arose from Filippo Maria having no offspring save an illegitimate daughter, Bianca. To the republic of Venice, which for several past decades had been engaged in a struggle with the duchy of Milan over the domination of northern Italy, the approaching death of Filippo Maria suggested the idea of appropriating Milan by seizure the moment the duke had departed this life. Obsessed with this plan, the republic refused to take seriously a counter-claim put out by Francesco Sforza. Sforza was a low-born peasant, who by making himself the foremost condottiere of Italy had become a political figure that could not be lightly brushed aside. Although, in order not to fall into dependency on a single too powerful general, Duke Filippo Maria had made it a practice to shift his favor from one condottiere to another, he had nonetheless come to lean so heavily on Francesco Sforza that he simply could not go on with his program of conquest without Sforza's support.

In this uncertain and fluctuating situation it was not surprising that the rude condottiere, Francesco Sforza, should have hatched a plan to marry Bianca with a view to claiming the succession on the death of Bianca's father by hereditary right. At the first communication of the marriage project to the highborn duke he flew into a rage, which cooled down, however, in measure as he realized his military impotence without the adventurer's support. In November, 1441, he let himself at length be persuaded to permit the marriage to take place by which the hireling soldier was convinced he had smoothed his path to the throne. The hope was not promptly realized for the double reason that Filippo Maria remained as instinctively hostile to the peasant-upstart after as before his acceptance of him as his daughter's husband, and that Venice stood on the alert to leap on Milan from across the border the moment the news reached it of the duke's demise.

The long-awaited death occurred at last on August 13, 1447, and its first effect was the defeat of both the stealthy plotters: in a sudden access of democratic delirium the people of Milan re-established their ancient republic! But since delirium is evanescent and a painfully inadequate foundation for a republic or any other kind of state, bitter divisions among the citizens followed, and the rival claimants, Sforza and the Venetian merchant oligarchy, had no difficulty in edging their way into the game. There followed a three-cornered struggle which, after three years of turmoil, was won by the hardy condottiere. In February, 1450, Francesco Sforza was acclaimed as their duke by the Milanese people in succession to the deceased last scion of the Visconti line.

In the hotly contested, prolonged Milanese succession struggle Cosimo de' Medici had from the start played an important, albeit invisible, role. As soon as it became reasonably clear that on Filippo Maria's death Milan would fall either to Sforza or to the state of Venice, Cosimo's mind had been made up. The duchy of Milan added to the republic of St. Mark would give the latter a political preponderance which would reduce Florence and the rest of the peninsula to effective subservience. He therefore throughout the many years the decision hung in the balance gave Sforza his support, which meant, in view of Sforza's inadequate financial resources, that he sustained the condottiere with an uninterrupted flow of subsidies. To this drain of funds the Florentines made powerful objection first, because no more than any people that has ever lived did they relish being taxed in an alien cause, and second, having for several generations suffered indignities at the hands of the Milanese duchy, they were vengefully delighted to have it swallowed up by Venice. In sign of Cosimo's readiness to stand his ground in a matter involving the existence of the state even to the point of risking a revolutionary rising, he backed the peasant-soldier until he issued from the struggle as the crowned duke of Milan.

A foreseen but unavoidable consequence for Cosimo of his support of Sforza against Venice was the replacement of the latter's seasoned friendship with its bitter enmity. Persisting in its war with Sforza even after his installation as duke, the angry merchant republic sought and obtained the alliance of Naples. Since this move obliged Florence to enter the struggle openly on Milan's side, all Italy blazed up in war—the usual trifling war of states operating with hired armies—until there fell on the combatants with the sound of doom the news of the capture of Constantinople by the Turks. The fateful event occurred on May 29, 1453. It gave pause to the Italian states, great and small alike, but, above all, to sea-girt Venice, which drew its very life-blood from the lands which the Turks were progressively flooding. Discussions inaugurated between Venice and Milan led in 1454 to the peace of Lodi, which Florence and Naples then accepted after a brief delay. When practically all the remaining states added their names to the Lodi agreement, it assumed in vague outline something of the appearance of an Italian confederation and was given an unusually solemn character by a paragraph whereby the signatories pledged themselves to a policy of peace and to the taking of united action against any member state guilty of disturbing it.

Lodi failed as a general league of peace for the same reason that has wrecked all similar peace leagues before and after that time. That reason was that each signatory continued to claim an unlimited sovereignty and passionately refused to accept any check on his pursuit of purposes calculated to promote his own aggrandizement. Consequently, Italy continued to be torn with rivalries and harassed with wars. Against this contentious background Florence stood forth as the only government that took the Lodi pledge to heart and actually got a little measurable profit from its stand. Its enlightened policy was due exclusively to Cosimo, effectively the city's ruler and actually its foreign minister. His twenty-year experience as head of the state that lay behind him at the time of Lodi had taught this circumspect statesman, whose leading trait was moderation, that a commercial republic like Florence was not adapted to the successful pursuit of war, and that the accommodation best suited to its character and needs was the Lodi federation pledged to the maintenance of peace on the basis of existing boundaries. As far as circumstances permitted, Cosimo henceforth made this purely defensive program his lode-star and had the immense satisfaction of thereby securing peace to Florence for the remainder of his rule. Nor is that the whole story of his achievement. His peace policy was taken over by his son, Piero, and, after a single, almost fatal lapse, by his grandson, Lorenzo, and in large part explains the high authority enjoyed by Florence during the period of these three outstanding Medici.

Owing to the close interaction at Florence as everywhere else of events abroad and at home, it came about that the pacification of Italy, sketched rather than effected at Lodi, produced the first movement of revolt against Cosimo's control since his assumption of power. A group of his adherents, encouraged by the prospect of peninsular security, came to the conclusion that they might now risk relaxing their domestic control by sacrificing the ten accoppiatori who handpicked the officials from among the eligible names in the borse. So bitterly were these high-riding manipulators resented by the whole population that they were stigmatized in common parlance as the ten tyrants. The plotters against Cosimo were his leading rivals in the Medicean party, with men like Luca Pitti, Agnolo Acciauoli, and Diotisalvi Neroni at their head. The hope that cemented their rebellion was that they would advance their own credit with the people while lowering that of Cosimo if, after first openly advocating the abolition of the accoppiatori, they would then succeed in bringing it about.

The mild Cosimo, ever eager to avoid conflict within the party, put no obstacle in the way of the dissidents, and before 1454, the year of the Lodi peace, had come to an end, the accoppiatori had been abolished and a return effected to the system of election by lot. Great was the jubilation of the Florentine citizenry over the reform and deep the satisfaction of the successful rebels. Before long, however, their joy was turned to apprehension from the circumstance that the signories created by lot exhibited a steadily mounting tendency to independence. When a signory at length was elected which proposed to draw up a new catasto as the basis for a general revision of the taxes, the plotters completely reversed themselves and loudly lamented their too precipitate lifting of the accoppiatori control.

To understand their changed attitude let us go back to the famous reform of 1427 which created an income tax on a theoretically equitable basis. This did not hinder its application, as had ever been the case in Florence, from being secretly so manipulated that the adherents of the party in power paid less and their opponents paid more than their fair share. Another irregularity arose from the failure to carry out the provision of the law that the catasto should be revised every three years. In consequence of neglecting the periodic reassessment the income tax levied in the middle fifties was still based on the catasto of 1432, and this illegal state of affairs enjoyed the favor of the leading Mediceans because, as men prevailingly of recent and steadily increasing wealth, they would not be smitten with the steeper tax resulting from a revised catasto.

As there was immense popular enthusiasm for revision, which the wary Cosimo refused to dampen, a new catasto was ordered for the year 1458, in spite of all that the repentant rebels could do to hinder it. But they had now had enough and more than enough of the uncontrolled signories they had wished on themselves and eagerly ran to Cosimo to implore him to restore the accoppiatori as their only shield against additional and worse surprises. We can imagine the slow, inscrutable smile with which the now ageing master of politics received their importunities. To impress the moral of the episode as deeply as possible on his slippery friends he kept them whining at his door-step for several months. Then only did he give permission to have the parliament summoned for the familiar sinister purpose of revising the law according to the interest of the ruling sect.

The meeting of the "reforming" parliament was set for August 11, 1458, and into what a constitutional travesty the ancient assembly of the people had by this time been transformed was masterfully illustrated by an account of its action sent to Francesco Sforza, duke of Milan, on August 8, that is, *three days anterior to the event*. The account was dispatched by Sforza's Florentine ambassador, who must have had it direct from Cosimo, the cynical impresario of the comedy. According to this communication on the morning of August 11, the troops of the government would occupy the piazza, only Medicean partisans would be permitted to join the assembly, the signory would offer the names of a commission empowered to "reform" the laws, the planted partisans would vigorously signify their approval and—the undoing of the accoppiatori would be again undone and the ten tyrants restored to their former authority! It must have given Cosimo much quiet satisfaction that the gonfalonier whose office it was to preside over this legislative mockery was none other than Luca Pitti, his chief rival within the party and the chief agitator four years before against the accoppiatori, of whose restoration he now stood forth as the leading advocate.

With Luca Pitti so steadily in the public view in the post-Lodi years many feather-brained Florentines inclined to the opinion that he was gradually replacing Cosimo at the head of the party. Not only had Luca recently prospered in business and acquired great wealth but, a vain and garrulous old man given to ostentatious display, he had begun a palace for himself on the slopes of the hill of San Giorgio on the left bank of the Arno which was laid out on a scale completely dwarfing the palace of his party chief. The Pitti palace, not completed till a much later time, still stands and invites comparison with the smaller but certainly imposing Medici palace, which is also still in existence. In many Florentine eyes the vast edifice laid out by Luca was additional evidence of a waxing rivalry between him and Cosimo in which Luca was visibly surging to the front. Perhaps the most remarkable feature of the reputed contest was that it never even for a moment troubled the older man's sleep. With his penetrating knowledge of our human kind he had taken the measure of the busy, self-important Luca and correctly viewed him as the ephemeral butterfly he was. True, Cosimo was now sloping to his end and, seriously crippled by gout, only rarely appeared in public; but neither he nor any other Florentine capable of looking beneath the surface enter-

tained the least doubt as to who it was that was sitting at the
controls of the ship of state.

Cosimo was visited with many private sorrows in his closing
years, but before we speak of them and essay a final estimate of
his life and character, we shall have to turn to the cultural side
of his activity with a view to assessing its significance for the
total movement of Florentine art and letters.

VI

COSIMO AS PATRON OF LETTERS AND ART

THE subject matter of this chapter, Cosimo's patronage of letters and of art, proved a leading occasion for the sharply divided judgment concerning him and his successors entertained, as we noted at the outset, by historians of the period. Native historians, in the main, concentrated on the politician and ignored the patron, foreign historians concentrated on the patron and ignored the politician. If we now consider the powerful bias of each group, in the light of which Cosimo's countrymen saw him as the traducer of his country's "liberty," saw him, that is, as evil, and the foreigners as the fountainhead of a famous culture, that is, as good, the wide spread between their respective estimates becomes intelligible. With the gradual weakening of the ancient prejudices on the advancing trail of modern scholarship a better balanced presentation has become possible and is the motivating principle of this book.

On the occasion of the General Council of 1439 Cosimo was moved, as mentioned in that connection, to weigh a plan for an academy of Platonic studies, which untoward circumstances then obliged him to abandon. Already fifty years old at the time, he would never have revolved a project so intimately expressive of the new learning, had he not long been familiar with its essential nature and general aims. Looking back, we can see that his having been born in Florence sufficed of itself to expose him from early boyhood to an influence with which the very air he breathed was saturated. But the attuning of his mind to the world of antiquity was not left to the accident of birth; for, though the son of a merchant destined to a merchant career, he was given express instruction in classical literature by several of its adepts. It thus came about that, without aspiring to professional mastery, he nursed a genuine interest in the movement. This, strengthened by innumerable personal contacts, cast him for the role of patron of the new learning, a role his wealth then permitted him to play in the lavish manner of a great prince.

From early manhood, and while his father still lived, he was already in close touch with representatives of the exciting new studies and was eagerly sought out by them for the support of their projects. However, it was not until his father's death and his assumption of the headship of the family that his patronage took on the munificent character that has made it famous. It deserves to be noted in passing that his younger brother, Lorenzo, seconded these efforts with a discriminating patronage of his own. But, owing to his inborn modesty and to the free recognition on his part of his older brother's superior endowment, he observed also in the field of culture the subordination which he had adopted at an early age and never ceased to practice in the political field. It was a grievous loss for Cosimo when the kindly and devoted Lorenzo died, at the age of forty-five, only six years after their return from a common exile.

Since the pursuit of classical scholarship brought no pecuniary reward except through an occasional and, usually, very temporary lectureship, its none too numerous patrons were perpetually importuned for free gifts. Of the sums distributed by Cosimo on this score no record is available, nor can it be ascertained what monies he allocated to the search for manuscripts buried in the decaying monasteries of Europe under the dust of centuries. That he gave liberally for both these purposes is sure, as it is also certain that he was interested in having the rare existent manuscripts systematically multiplied by expert copyists.

These closely related activities awakened the desire for books of his own, for a well-stocked library, and with such a library in process of formation so public-spirited a citizen as Cosimo would begin to debate with himself how to make it available for the steadily expanding company of the learned. The stages in the evolution of this particular interest can be concretely illustrated by what happened to the books assembled by an older friend of Cosimo's, Niccolò Niccoli by name. This Niccolò, who began life as a merchant, became so enamored of books and the new learning, that he closed his shop and devoted himself to his hobby with the singlemindedness of an old-time Benedictine monk. He succeeded in collecting some eight hundred volumes, a number probably unrivaled in his day and made possible, in part at least, by Niccolò's having been at pains to acquire a fine handwriting in order to serve at need as his own professional scribe. When this knowledge-bitten ex-merchant died—the year was 1437—he was a bankrupt and his books would have been dispersed to pay his debts, had not Cosimo intervened. He satisfied his friend's obligations, got title to his books, and then took up the problem of their most advantageous disposition. Engaged at the time in restoring in the form with which it is still invested the monastery of San Marco, he ordered the architect Michelozzo to make provision therein for a structure suitable for the housing of Niccolò's treasures. By the year 1444 their transfer to their new home could be effected and the library of San Marco be opened as the first public institution of its kind in Europe. That it develop into a lively and expanding and not settle into a barren and frozen repository Cosimo added to its original core from time to time as long as he lived.

Nor is that the whole story of the open-handed Cosimo's activity as the founder of libraries. As soon as his construction of the abbey buildings at San Domenico under Fiesole had reached the necessary stage, he resolved to supply a stock of books and, according to the book-dealer, Vespasiano da Bisticci, consulted him on the quickest manner to obtain it. If we are to believe this same book-crazed but honest and credible gossip, he met Cosimo's wishes by hiring forty-five scribes and with their aid was able to deliver two hundred volumes in the course of the next twenty-two months. Apparently requiring the intellectual stimulus created by books for contented daily living, Cosimo assembled a third library, which he housed in his fine new palace in the *via Larga*. But this, although opened freely to his friends, was not dedicated to public use.

The roster of humanists with whom Cosimo came into direct contact includes practically all the outstanding members of the tribe. In their vast majority they remained staunchly devoted to him, which, in view of the sordid greed they all exhibited in varying degree, admits of no other interpretation than that he never ceased to favor them with his patronage. He was particularly close to Leonardo Bruni (d. 1444) and Poggio Bracciolini (d. 1459), both of whom rose, on Cosimo's express invitation, to be chancellors of the Florentine republic and who, in addition to their prescriptive labors in philology, distinguished themselves by numerous contributions of a literary character revealing the classical orientation of their authors. For later generations at least the most memorable achievement each of them has to his credit was the composition of a history of the city he officially served. Of course they composed their histories, as everything else they wrote, in the Latin language in the rock-ribbed conviction that it was the only medium worthy of the indubitable descendants of the vanished Roman conquerors.

Considered as a group, the humanists displayed the vanity

and intellectual arrogance which have been only too commonly the attributes of self-centered and world-removed closet-scholars through the ages. If anything, however, the fifteenth century scholars surpassed in these unpleasant traits their professional kin of every preceding and every subsequent period as well and achieved a savagery of vituperative personal abuse which stands as an unequaled record. The behavior pattern to which they conformed clearly reveals them as sycophants and parasites, and we might incline to sweep them from the boards with a single contemptuous gesture, if we did not remind ourselves that under the social and political conditions prevailing in their time they were obliged to comport themselves as they did in order to come by the minimum income they required to perform their invaluable service.

Although Cosimo had no direct connection with these professional brawls, he could not entirely escape them either, and in one instance at least was indecently sprayed with the turpitude which was their pervasive element. A leading scholar of the day was Francesco Filelfo, who rose to high honor by reason of his extensive travels in Greece and the valuable studies resulting from his exceptional enterprise. Born in the papal states in 1389, he had in the course of the wanderings imposed on his kind by their unceasing search for a livelihood, settled at Florence in the days of the Albizzi supremacy. The situation made him something of an Albizzi adherent, in any case more of an adherent than was good for him on the return of the Medici brothers from exile. It is not worth while to go into the chicanery with which he then found himself beset, if not at the direct instance of Cosimo, certainly not without his knowledge. The result was that he abandoned Florence in high dudgeon and took revenge for his discomfiture by discharging against Cosimo a pamphlet of unrivaled abuse. Among the Medicean's numerous humanist dependents it was Poggio who undertook to repay Filelfo in kind. The rare readers of this exchange of literary slops agree that it was scurrility at its lowest and vilest. That

Cosimo was bespattered by the flying bilge is undeniable but he bore it with dignity. The only reason for mentioning the one clamorous humanist feud in which he became involved is to bring home to us the often inhumanly degraded atmosphere enveloped in which the great liberating work of the classical revival proceeded.

It is probable that the greatest satisfaction that came to Cosimo from his association with scholars is connected with the name of Marsilio Ficino. Marsilio was the son of his physician who, plunging with obsessive fervor into the new studies, fell presently under the spell of Plato. It was a heavy drawback that he did not command the Greek language and that to learn it would require more years of study than his father could afford to pay for. At this point Cosimo, pleased with the young man's ardor, came forward with an offer of assistance. It took the form of a money allowance supplemented with a farm near his own villa of Careggi, where the young scholar could follow his studies in the congenial solitude of nature. In return for these benefits Marsilio pledged himself to devote his life to Plato with the final purpose of crowning his labors by making the great Athenian's contributions to philosophy available in the Latin language.

Cosimo's life was already nearing its close when these arrangements were made. The deep contentment they caused him arose from the fact that he was thus belatedly providing for the Platonic Academy which he had dreamed of in the far days of Gemistus Plethon's visit to Florence and which he had been obliged to abandon for lack of scholarly support. True, the development of the Academy would have to wait on the growth of Marsilio Ficino to his full mental stature. Fortunately Cosimo lived long enough to become convinced that the little farm in which he had installed his young friend would nurse a spark, from which in the days of his descendants a beacon would be lighted visible from end to end of the peninsula.

+

Cosimo As Patron of Letters and Art

Of all the nobler arts of man the oldest, most inclusive, and also most indispensable, is architecture. Wherefore it is not surprising that the young Cosimo de' Medici lent an eager ear when Filippo Brunelleschi inaugurated his campaign against the current Gothic style of construction and advocated a return to the abandoned principles of classicism. The novel, exciting message reached even Cosimo's father, old Giovanni di Bicci, who commissioned the innovator to rebuild the sacristy of San Lorenzo in the style he championed. Brunelleschi was occupied to the limit of his strength at the time with raising the giant cupola over the east end of the cathedral of Santa Maria del Fiore and continued at his task for fourteen unbroken years till its completion in 1434. Notwithstanding his absorption with the cupola, he accepted Giovanni's commission and, when Giovanni died before the sacristy was finished, yielded to the request of Cosimo, the new family head, to bring it to completion. Because the soaring cupola was chiefly an engineering feat and conformed neither to Gothic nor classical principles, the sacristy of San Lorenzo constitutes the earliest structure fully illustrative of the new style. It has all the proper appointments—pilasters (in place of columns), Corinthian capitals, entablature, and frieze—studied from classical remains and has besides that balance and serenity which provide their total meaning in sharp distinction from the restlessness and aspiration expressive of true Gothic.

After the sacristy of San Lorenzo had received the bodies of the parents of Cosimo he turned to the far greater and more costly enterprise of reconstructing the church of which the sacristy was a minor feature and naturally assigned the undertaking to the admired builder of the sacristy. Many years passed before the church was completed; but when the scaffoldings were at last removed, it at once took its place as the most distinguished example of quattrocento architecture within the city's limits. Again let us note that it fully meets the new architectural formula in that it is supported on rows of slender columns, that it is lighted by arched windows above the columns of the nave, and that the nave itself terminates vertically in a rich, geometrically coffered ceiling. To pass from the ponderous vaults and deep shadows of Santa Maria del Fiore to the clear, calculated proportions of San Lorenzo is to step from the medieval world of values into that of the Renaissance.

One other church built at Cosimo's orders has been commonly attributed to Brunelleschi. It is the abbey church, called *La Badia,* at San Domenico below Fiesole. The hesitation in ascribing it to Brunelleschi arises from the fact that it was not erected until after the famous architect's death. However, so definitely does it carry the hallmarks of his style that it may with complete confidence be referred to a design which Brunelleschi had elaborated but did not live long enough to execute. When Cosimo resolved to build himself a new residence in Florence, he naturally referred the matter to his earliest architectural guide. However, when Brunelleschi submitted a wooden model foreshadowing a structure of extraordinary magnitude and splendor, Cosimo rejected it on the characteristic ground that its execution would excite an undesirable envy and mark him as aspiring to that open tyranny which his enemies were always proclaiming as his final goal. Brunelleschi was a diminutive, peppery, and high-spirited man. Vasari reports the characteristic touch that promptly on learning of Cosimo's decision he smashed his model to bits (*in mille pezzi*). The incident ended with the banker-statesman's adopting for his residence the much more modest project of Michelozzo Michelozzi.

While the Medici palace which Michelozzi completed in the early forties was on a much meaner scale than the one projected by Brunelleschi, it was still a very imposing affair. It was erected on the broadest street of the city, the via Larga, within stone's throw of the San Lorenzo complex which the Medici family had taken under its wing. Florentine private dwellings accorded with a tradition which forbade the adoption of either a strict Gothic or a strict Renaissance style. From the earliest times of

the commune structures of this sort had, on account of the
prevalence of violent family feuds, to be planned with regard
not only to the needs of housing but also to those of defense.
If by the fifteenth century the family feuds had largely become
a thing of the past, class riots and political upheavals were still
so common that, whenever an individual citizen could afford
the outlay, he continued to build with an eye to protection. In
these circumstances it was inescapable that the new residence
planned by Cosimo should meet the traditional defense require-
ment, although it would be permissible, and even desirable, to
have it also reflect the greater measure of public security which
had come to prevail.

Of these somewhat complicated factors Michelozzi's Medici
palace is a perfect expression. It rises to the height of three
stories, the first bristling with immense, rough-hewn stone
blocks, which invited assault with a confident air. Originally
there was a single arched gate set in the center of this quarried
mass, to recover the lost effect of which we must use our imagination and obliterate the row of arched windows at the gate
level which are a much later addition. The second and third
stories, which served as the family's living quarters, communicate their more domestic character by being constructed of
smaller fashioned, smooth-faced stones. A further softening
effect is achieved by the three stories being set off by continuous
horizontal moldings. This touch of organization is repeated in
the long rows of mullioned windows and the boldly projecting
roof which sets the building in a solid frame. On passing through
the gate the fortress concept, which still largely dominates the
exterior, vanishes entirely, and we enter a court open to the sky
which, since we are now enfolded by the security of the new
age, is invested with classical elegance by means of a ground-
floor gallery of graceful columns and rows of mullioned windows lining the two upper stories.

As attached to Michelozzi as to Brunelleschi, Cosimo, on resolving to rebuild the old Dominican monastery of San Marco,

entrusted the work to the younger man with the happiest consequences. We have already heard of the hall-like chamber which Michelozzi built and Cosimo dedicated as the first public library of the western world. But the outstanding and memorable feature of the rebuilt monastery is its cloister. It is to this day a favorite haunt of the more impressionable visitors of the Arno city, who are in complete agreement that there is no pleasanter retreat within its compass than the pillared inner gallery of San Marco with its broad walk of echoing flagstones.

We conclude the story of Cosimo, the builder, with the record of his villas. His most usual and favorite country retreat was Careggi. It went back to his father and lay within easy reach of the city's western gate. Cosimo added a villa at Cafaggiolo in the Mugello, the original home of his race, and was at pains to make more habitable an older castellated structure at Trebbio higher up in the mountains. A country residence on the upper slopes of Fiesole was begun by him but was not completed until after his time. It is worth mentioning, because it defines the gradual consolidation of the position of the family, that none of the structures treated in this chapter, whether public or residential, was completed without often considerable intermissions. Even the great city palace was not from the start the massive cube of stone that now overwhelms the observer. A woodcut which Poliziano incorporated in his *Commentary on the Pazzi Conspiracy*, published in 1478, shows that at that date it had not yet achieved its familiar final proportions.

The fifteenth century movement in the arts constitutes an early Renaissance phase commonly given the Italian name of quattrocento. Literally four hundred, it refers to the fifteenth century which the Italians call the four hundred century. As is not unusual in similar instances of historical unfolding, the developments which sum up quattrocento art have been so squeezed together for the sake of convenience by writers of the field that they would appear to have come to sudden explosive birth as at the summons of some master magician. In the case of architecture this magicianship was credited to Filippo Brunelleschi, in that of sculpture to Donatello, and in that of painting to Masaccio. The compressed pattern has won such general acceptance that it could not fail to draw a bow of recognition from the author of this book.

However, on now taking up Cosimo de' Medici's relation to the sculpture of the period and obliged in this connection to look somewhat more closely into the matter of origins, we cannot but be struck with the fact that the assigning of the role of sole initiator to Donatello reveals itself as one of those summations by which an involved subject matter is reduced to a handy formula but which cannot survive a disinterested probing of the actual circumstances. While it is undebatable that Donatello gave a stronger impulse to the development of quattrocento sculpture than any of his contemporaries, it suffices to turn to Vasari's account of the episode that inaugurated the new movement to be supplied with convincing proof that Donatello was not its earliest representative.

From the first and still unsurpassed and indispensable historian of the Fine Arts we learn that in the year 1401 the city of Florence invited a competition open to all Italy for a pair of bronze doors for the northern entrance to the baptistery of San Giovanni to serve as a companion-piece, long overdue, to the bronze doors of the southern entrance completed in 1336 by Andrea Pisano. Continues Vasari (greatly condensed): From among the sculptors who presented themselves, seven were chosen, three of them Florentines and the rest Tuscans, each of whom received a sum of money for living expenses on the understanding that he would re-appear when a year had passed with a bronze panel of the same size as those which composed Andrea Pisano's earlier doors. It was stipulated that the subject to be treated should be Abraham's sacrifice of Isaac. Promptly at the appointed time the seven competitors reported with their handiwork to await the judgment of the consuls of the guild of merchants and such other citizens as the consuls had invited to serve with them as jurors. And in spite of a lively difference of opinion due to each panel's having a distinct and individual merit, it was agreed that the renditions of Filippo Brunelleschi and Lorenzo Ghiberti were outstanding. Whereupon Brunelleschi and his young friend, Donatello, drawing aside, concluded that Ghiberti's piece was so well designed and its figures turned with so much grace that it would be invidious not to give him the award.

Vasari's dragging Donatello into the picture is definitely an error, since Donatello cannot have participated in the competition for the sufficient reason that he was at the time only fifteen years old. Fortunately the two admittedly pre-eminent panels of Brunelleschi and Ghiberti have come down to us, making credible the praise they both elicited as well as the preference that was finally accorded to Ghiberti's work. From a purely historical angle the striking thing about the two pieces is that they have alike cast off the medieval shackles and leave not the shadow of a doubt that they are the products of a new spirit compounded of a return to classicism and a fresh approach to nature. It is therefore clear that quattrocento sculpture did not have either Donatello or any one of his slightly older contemporaries as its parent but that, in the manner of spiritual transformations through the ages, it came to practically simultaneous expression among the many studios of the Florentine area at the turn of the century. Nor is there any escape from the conclusion that quattrocento architecture and painting came to birth in the same manner and that in last analysis we are confronted in these artistic novelties with a general forward movement of society. While this is important background information, it does not reduce by a measurable shade the merit inhering in the initiative supplied by leading individuals.

Returning to Cosimo and his response to the new sculptural outburst, we note the indubitable fact of his close attachment to Donatello. Not that he denied his patronage to Ghiberti, of whom we may assume so absorbing a concern with the doors of San Giovanni that he had little or no time left for other commissions. In simple fact Ghiberti remained so devotedly and uninterruptedly in the service of the baptistery that when, after twenty years, the North Doors had been completed, the enthusiasm which they aroused caused him to be entrusted also with the East Doors facing the cathedral. The two sets of bronze doors between them engaged the master's energies for no less than forty-nine years, from 1403 to 1452. This means that he labored on them throughout his life as an artist, since he was still a very young man when he won the famous competition of 1401 and lived only three years after seeing the East Doors swung into place on their massive hinges. The later doors exhibit an advance not only in modeling and composition but also in the technical mastery of a peculiarly stubborn material. It was to them that Michelangelo addressed the unstinted praise that they were worthy to serve as the gates of paradise. In his engrossing labor on the two sets of doors lies the explanation that there is certain record of but a single commission carried out by Ghiberti at Cosimo's request. This was the handsome metal reliquary intended for the reception of the bones of three obscure martyrs and now preserved in a Florentine museum.

Perhaps because of his kindly nature, perhaps because of his peasant-like simplicity, it was Donatello who among all the sculptors of the quattrocento proved pre-eminently to be Cosimo's man. His wide artistic range will promptly reveal itself to whoever juxtaposes the Saint George (once in a niche of Or San Michele but now in the Museo Nazionale) and the King David which still looks down on the busy traffic of the cathedral square from its niche high in Giotto's tower. The fully armored Saint George is the perfectly achieved expression of idealistic and dedicated young manhood, whereas King David is an uncompromisingly literal representation of an awkwardly shuffling, decrepit old baldhead. Refusing to see the warrior king of Israel in this fugitive from the almshouse and vastly amused by his completely hairless pate, the Florentines laughingly dubbed him *lo Zuccone* or Pumpkinhead. Between these two contradictory and yet often merged directives of his art lies Donatello's total work embracing such memorable creations as the St. Mark in a niche of Or San Michele, the Mary Magdalene of wood in the baptistery, the organ loft of dancing children for the cathedral, and the imposing bronze equestrian statue of the condottiere, Gattamelata, which dominates a public square of Padua and which is the first equestrian statue in metal fashioned since the far days of Rome.

Since this book is the story of the Medici and only incidentally that of the arts, we shall abandon our brief digression on the range of Donatello's work to consider the labors he performed at the special urgency of Cosimo. Vasari informs us that the friendly ruler kept him constantly engaged (*di continuo lo faceva lavorare*) and in the course of his narrative account of Donatello's life lists more commissions than we can spare space to enumerate. Outstanding are those concerned with the Medicean church of San Lorenzo and the Medicean palace. For the sacristy of San Lorenzo built by his good friend, Brunelleschi, the sculptor did a wash basin, the stucco ornaments of the frieze, a bronze door with figures in low relief, and four saints, of which Saints Lorenzo and Stephen deserve particular mention. For the courtyard of the palace he decorated the frieze over the arches of the gallery with eight charming medallions copied from ancient cameos and medals. He added a beautifully modeled David in bronze, which on the fall of the Medici in 1494, began an odyssey, which, after many adventures, terminated in our day in the Museo Nazionale.

No longer able to work in his declining years, Donatello became the pensioner of Cosimo, who, on his death, bequeathed him a small farm in the Mugello region. To Vasari, one of whose charms is the never failing human touch, we owe a story, which may fittingly close this meager note on a great artist, since it reveals the childlike simplicity which was the kernel of his being. Before a year had gone following Cosimo's bequest, the old sculptor appeared at the door of the Medici palace to ask that the farm be taken back. He could not keep it, he said, because the peasant who worked it gave him no peace. One day he would show up with the complaint that the wind had blown down the dove-cote, on another that the government had seized his cattle for back taxes, and on still another that a storm had ruined his vines and olive trees. A small cash annuity, he let it be modestly inferred, was infinitely preferable.

Useful and even indispensable as periodization is, it should not be permitted to obscure the fact that, since change is uninterrupted and continuous, a too rigid periodization seriously distorts the true situation. To illustrate: although it is undeniable that the medieval principles of art were in due time completely crowded out by the new Renaissance principles, the passage from the earlier to the later outlook was effected so gradually that a transition period regularly intervened, wherein the old and the new practices existed side by side without any uneasy evidence of incompatibility.

This situation is admirably disclosed by Fra Angelico, with whom we begin our review of quattrocento painting. Born a simple and deeply conservative peasant, Fra Angelico at an early age became a Dominican friar and took up the practice of painting in the medieval spirit of unwavering devotion to God and his saints. If he did not follow the more mundane tradition of the authoritative Giotto, it was because, according to Fra Angelico's particular understanding of Christianity, the painter's single mission was to proclaim the goodness of God and of God's creation. To this end he resorted to delicate, high-keyed colors which make his works shine with an opaline luster and utter celestial song. We might define him as a belated medievalist, individually distinct from all his predecessors, were it not that, doing his work in the first half of the fifteenth century—

he died in 1455—he did not fail to absorb some of the technical advances of the quattrocento, while refusing to take over as much as a trace of its secular outlook. In short, he was a transition figure with a message of religious ecstasy which derived straight from *il poverello* of Assisi, the sainted Francis, and which has lost none of its freshness after the passage of five hundred years.

When Cosimo de' Medici undertook that reconstruction of the dilapidated Dominican monastery of San Marco of which mention has repeatedly been made, he came into intimate association with its prior and his flock of brothers, of whom Fra Angelico was one. In measure as the various structures of the monastery complex were completed, their decoration was intrusted to the painter-brother of already established fame. The whole history of art records no more fortunate conjunction of the right man with the right opportunity. Fra Angelico's luminous and moving frescos are encountered on every wall of San Marco, in the lunettes over the doors of the cloister, in the chapter house, and above all, two score and more of them, in the double row of monastic cells of the second story. To spend a morning among them is to be transported from this world of hunger, suffering, and strife to the hushed peace promised the faithful on passing to their final reward.

Although Fra Angelico was not blind to the technical improvements of the age, he profited little or nothing by the man who by universal consent takes rank with Giotto as the second founder of Florentine painting. This was Masaccio, who, dying in 1428, at twenty-seven years of age, was able, with his single fresco series in the Brancacci chapel to communicate an impulse which did not exhaust itself for a hundred years. A master of composition, Masaccio was also the master of the human form, to which he succeeded in giving the appearance of the three-dimensional solidity of sculpture.

To him all subsequent practitioners of painting, beginning with Fra Filippo Lippi (1406-1469), became in varying degree indebted. Fra Filippo was a light-minded brother of the Carmelite order at the opposite pole from Fra Angelico in that, unconcerned with the joys of heaven, he could never get his fill of the material joys of the good earth. He was the first Florentine painter to tell the gospel story in the simple terms of everyday experience. This conspicuous secularism made him a general favorite and seems to have been the leading reason for the attraction to his work and person manifested by Cosimo. Not only did he load the loose-living friar with commissions but he repeatedly intervened to shield him from the penalties which his wild escapades invited on the part both of his ecclesiastical superiors and the civil courts.

There were contemporaries worthier than Fra Filippo of the great banker's support, but it is not recorded that he reached out a hand to them. Conspicuous among them were Paolo Uccello (d. 1475) and Andrea del Castagno (d. 1457). They lacked Fra Filippo's engaging humanity but have the considerable merit of continued eager experimentation with the exciting, recently discovered technical devices, Uccello concerning himself more particularly with perspective, Andrea with anatomy. Their labors added greatly to the store of liberating knowledge assembled by the local studios but, owing to what we may call their scientific aloofness, they were not widely appreciated. Florentine painting did not reach its flood until Cosimo's scepter had passed first, to his son, Piero, and then, to his grandson, Lorenzo, both of whom, together with the rule of the city, freely took over also their predecessor's stimulating patronage of the arts.

VII

THE RULE OF PIERO

WITH advancing years Cosimo became afflicted with many ills, especially gout, and was periodically house-bound and bed-ridden, often for weeks at a time. In consequence he gave less attention to public affairs, and his party associates, with Luca Pitti at their head, were so much more in evidence at the palace of the priors that the opinion gained ground in some quarters that they had supplanted him. It was a judgment laughably wide of the mark, for Cosimo had, since his advent to power, accumulated such immense prestige both at home and abroad that his authority remained unthreatened, in spite of partial withdrawal and slackened energy.

Nor was the mildness that characterized his last years a signal departure from his earlier attitude. Cosimo was by nature a man moderate, humane, and averse to violence. While it is true that his government supplemented the good will on which it mainly rested with practices of fraud and force, this was the situation throughout Italy, with the distinction in favor of Florence, that the laws were less often suspended and the opposition less brutally dealt with than anywhere else. In spite of the irregularities and excesses which marked every stage of the history of the republic, an honorable tradition of citizenship had taken shape, to which Cosimo was pleased spontaneously to adhere. Consequently, although he was the effective master of Florence, he never for even a moment considered adopting the ostentatious trappings of the tyrants, who were sprouting in his time throughout the peninsula, or of setting himself apart from his fellow citizens by surrounding his person with a court and his palace with an armed guard. In appearance he might have passed for the typical Florentine trader, for he was of medium height, robust frame, with large, rude features in an olive-complexioned face. He habitually wore the long cloak of simple cut called *lucco*, the prescribed garment of the self-respecting citizen, and greeted the men and women of whatever station he encountered in the streets and market with the same easy familiarity. A manner less charged with aristocratic aloofness could not be imagined.

We noted in an earlier chapter how his intelligent decision to share the offices and dignities with the leaders of his party strengthened his position. Owing partly to his natural reticence, partly to his meager endowment as an orator, he kept himself habitually in reserve and sent his closest dependents into the political fray in his behalf. In the course of an agitated public life he became an expert on the subject of the human animal and its human, all too human behavior. Pungent evidence thereof was revealed by pointed comments, which he delivered from time to time and which the famed malice of the Florentines rolled like delicious morsels under the tongue. His enemies were prompt to adduce them as proof of his cold and calculating cynicism. While it is undeniable that they are abundantly cynical, they have a razor edge to them which reflects their author's wit and penetration. For their flavor let some of them be here set down: states are not maintained by pater nosters; two yards of red cloth suffice to create an honorable citizen; envy is a plant that should not be watered; better a city ruined than a city lost. Their epigramatic compression caused them to be incorporated in the local folk-lore, where they have endured to the present day.

Like all his mental traits and personal habits, Cosimo's Christian piety was a subject of sharp contention. His enemies represented it as pure hypocrisy and, in support of their claim, pointed to his generous patronage of humanism with its notorious pagan implications. In reply his friends listed the ecclesiastical edifices erected by his bounty, San Lorenzo, the Badia of Fiesole, the monastery of San Marco. The embittered debate was idle casuistry, for in Cosimo's case, as in that of most of the leading spirits of the age, the old and the new, Christianity and antiquity, managed to exist side by side without any disturbing conflict. At San Marco monastery Cosimo had a cell reserved to himself to which he retired from time to time in order to silence for a happy interval the disturbing tumult of the world. It is preposterous to assume that he periodically practiced prayer and penitence except to satisfy a genuine need of the heart.

To plumb Cosimo to the depth of his being is to find the merchant. Born to the merchant tradition, he played the merchant role with unrivaled success and quite possibly would never have entered politics, had he not been forced to do so in order to protect his merchant interest. It is true that on becoming head of the state he promptly proved that he commanded also the particular equipment required by the political game to which he had become committed. But regardless of his absorption by the cares of government, he never allowed them to divert him from the attention he owed to the original source of his power, the family bank. Possessed of shrewd caution and bold initiative in happy unison, he succeeded in so enlarging its operations, that it became the leading institution of its kind in the western world and brought the almost fabulous returns, which by enabling him to practice his bounteous patronage of art and letters, paid a welcome additional dividend by enhancing his political prestige.

His marriage with Contessina Bardi was a perfect expression of his merchant outlook, for the lady belonged to one of the most distinguished banking families of an older day. She presented him with two sons, Piero and Giovanni, who on marrying in their turn into merchant families, lived with their wives and children in the Medici palace in the manner of a close patriarchal clan. To the physical afflictions that weighed upon the ageing leader grievous personal anxieties added their toll. The only son of Giovanni died at an early age and was followed in 1463 by Giovanni himself. The older son, Piero, was so gravely plagued by the family malady of gout that, even as a young man, he was often completely incapacitated for a prolonged period. Piero had two promising boys, Lorenzo and Giuliano, but it would be some years before they would be able to assume responsibility either in the bank or in the government. The outstanding ambition of every true son of Florence was to leave behind a large and prosperous progeny. We may therefore entertain no doubt touching the regrets aroused in Cosimo by his limited and shrinking brood. It is related that, shortly after Giovanni's death, he had himself carried in his invalid's chair through the empty rooms of his great palace and that he let his grief escape in the muttered words: "Too large a house for so small a family."

In the spring of 1464 he insisted on his removal to his beloved villa at Careggi, where, on August 1, he died at the advanced age of seventy-five years. He was buried without special ceremonies but amidst a vast concourse of his fellow citizens before the high altar of the church of San Lorenzo, which owed its existence to his munificence. The plain slab over his tomb carries his name and under it the simple inscription: *Pater Patriae*. The concise epitaph was the tribute his sorrowing countrymen paid him under the immediate sting of their great loss.

And so Cosimo slept with his fathers and Piero ruled in his stead. Born in 1416, he had received an education which, while preparing him for a merchant career, provided him at the same time with more than a nodding acquaintance with the current intellectual interests. When it came to choosing a bride, he followed the example set by his father and, in strict accord with long established custom, married a woman of a leading native family, Lucrezia Tornabuoni by name. The Tornabuoni, like the Bardi, from among whom Cosimo had taken his wife, were a banking family more ancient than the Medici which had passed the crest of its fortunes and was visibly sloping to its decline.

Lucrezia Tornabuoni was a remarkable woman, the perfect embodiment, one is tempted to affirm, of the ancient Florentine ideal of wife and mother. In addition to the two sons already mentioned, Lorenzo and Giuliano, she bore her husband three daughters, Maria, Bianca, and Lucrezia, the last-named affectionately called Nannina in the family. All her children carried the mark of her influence through life, more particularly her son, Lorenzo, whose devotion to his mother was continuous and exemplary. In one respect she was the strict and competent ruler of the home commended in the Bible as arising betimes and looking well after the ways of the household; in another, she was the robed priestess charged with the preservation of all the ancient pieties of the tribe. From their childhood she so steeped her children in the beliefs and folkways of Catholicism that, in spite of the pagan influences that prevailed in their day, they never broke away from their Christian moorings. She resorted at times to poetry to give expression to her overflowing religious feelings, and the spiritual anchorage evidenced by her sentiments coupled with her notable practical intelligence made her the invaluable counselor of her husband in all his affairs.

The gout with which Piero was crippled from early manhood has been diagnosed by modern medical science as a particularly painful form of arthritis. Whatever it may in fact have been, it so frequently chained him to house and bed that his prolonged withdrawals from public view persuaded the older Florentine historians to rate him as a relatively unimportant link in the

Medicean succession. The opinion has undergone a substantial correction at the hands of recent investigators. His effective resolution of a serious political crisis to be presently related will speak for itself. Hardly less revealing was his excellent management of the family bank, the neglect and weakening of which would with mathematical certainty have brought down the towering political superstructure. Precisely as in the case of his father, Piero was by native genius primarily a trader with a trader's outlook on life. Thus prompted, he never took his eye off the bank with its numerous branches established in the leading commercial centers of the western world. Under his guidance, which, again like his father's, was a mixture of boldness and caution, its fortunes, and with them the family returns, reached the highest level they ever attained. The decline under the management of the far more brilliant Lorenzo, at some points of a positively catastrophic nature, will be taken up in due time.

Piero was an ardent bibliophile and followed in his father's footsteps as the buyer of books and the patron of libraries. He also came to the support of humanistic scholarship and gladly continued the benefactions to Marsilio Ficino, on whom rested the fortunes of the Platonic Academy in process of formation. Had his rule extended over the thirty-year span the fates afforded his father, he would almost certainly have duplicated his father's record as a promoter of learning. The brief five-year period he served as head of the government hardly enabled him to do more than to disclose his intentions.

The same may be said of his patronage of the arts. Between the two directions recently taken by Florentine painting Piero, like Cosimo, turned to the unpretentious, warm-hearted storytellers, of whom Fra Filippo Lippi was the earliest representative. A certain harshness about the experimental and more scholarly group, among whom Paolo Uccello and Andrea del Castagno figured as leaders, deprived them of popular appeal. An outstanding successor of the mundane and uncomplicated Fra

Filippo was Benozzo Gozzoli (1420-1498). On Piero's resolving appropriately to decorate the private chapel in the family palace, it was Gozzoli whom he selected for the undertaking. In view of the animated scenes with which the painter splashed those chapel walls and which have delighted all the succeeding generations from his time to our own, we are bound to agree that the master of the house could not have made a happier choice. While Gozzoli was in a general way of Fra Filippo's artistic persuasion, his worldliness sounded a different note from Fra Filippo's. It was his special bent to be drawn to the colorful processions and pageants by which the Florentines, and the Italians in general, were at that time expressing their conviction that a new spring had arrived for mankind and that the earth, in spite of all that the church might say to the contrary, was a goodly habitation.

A painting by Fra Filippo, which pictured the Virgin kneeling in adoration before her Son, had for some time adorned the altar of the otherwise bare little Medicean chapel. The task assigned to Gozzoli was to picture the splendid train of the Three Eastern Kings winding through the happy countryside spread over three walls of the chapel in order to lay their gifts at the feet of the Divine Child of the Fra Filippo painting on the altar representing the fourth wall and the goal of their pilgrimage. The magnificent continuous procession, done in fresco, is in admirable state of preservation and with its richly attired horsemen and footmen, with its garlands and banners, is an imaginative summation of all the triumphal processions that have ever been held on earth. The simple-hearted naturalism that Gozzoli shared with all the members of the school to which he belonged is interestingly betrayed by his introducing carefully portraitized members of the Medici family together with a large number of lesser contemporaries, including himself, into the vast pageant which, presumably passing over the hills of Judaea, was in reality making its way over the familiar beloved landscape of Tuscany.

+

On the invalided Piero assuming the reins of government there was a movement of unrest in the Medicean opposition which had come to life in Cosimo's last period. Its leading figures were Luca Pitti, Diotisalvi Neroni, and Agnolo Acciaiuoli, ambitious men all and not without some measure of capacity. Their difficulty was that, while deeply persuaded that they deserved to be enjoying more authority than they were exercising, they were unable to agree on a plan of action possessed of something of a popular appeal. At a loss how best to proceed, they permitted the initiative to pass to a fourth member of their group whose interest in politics was not, like their own, limited to a lively sense of personal advantage. This was Niccolò Soderini. Correctly enough Niccolò ascribed the control exercised by the Medici to the device of the accoppiatori; but much less correctly he had also persuaded himself that the return to election by lot would suffice to restore the "liberty" his fellow citizens had never ceased to cherish.

A man of flaming emotions and a born orator, Niccolò was able to sweep the councils off their feet when in September, 1465, he inaugurated his campaign with an attack on the hated constitutional excrescence invented by the Medici. His success automatically restored the earlier election by lot; and when, on the following November 1, the drawings took place for the November-December signory, lo and behold, Niccolò Soderini emerged as gonfalonier of Justice, for it was his name that leaped from the professedly free and unmanipulated borse. It was clear evidence, if such was needed, what the "liberty" was like which he had so eloquently insisted was inherent in the older system. A cheering crowd of vast proportions attended the new head of the state to the seat of the government in the palace with the enthusiastic demonstration reaching its climax when an olive wreath was dramatically planted on the liberator's brow.

Niccolò was a well-meaning idealist with little knowledge of men and less of practical politics. During his incumbency of the gonfalonierat he proposed to the councils numerous constitutional changes, warmly recommended as "reforms," which these bodies regularly rejected. Overwhelmingly Medicean in sentiment, they were not averse to a modest clipping of the family's wings, but they showed no inclination whatever in favor of a radical revolution under the leadership of an impractical dreamer. When Niccolò's term ended at the close of his second month of office, he slunk unattended and uncheered to the obscurity of his home, a sadder but, alas, not a wiser man. In fact he permitted himself to become so embittered that he no longer scrupled to revolve plans for the forceful ejection of the Medici from the city. In this mood he drew close to the three fellow oligarchs, whose long hesitations at length broke down under the impact of Niccolò's inflamed resolution.

The anti-Medicean revolt now hatched by the four Medicean rebels was greatly favored by an event at Milan. On March 8, 1466, died the doughty condottiere, Francesco Sforza, who, some sixteen years before, had crowned a career of violence by making himself duke of Milan. Since his son, Galeazzo Maria, was a young man of twenty, inexperienced and without a trace of his father's varied talents, it was far from certain that he would succeed in imposing his authority. The succession crisis gravely disquieted Piero de' Medici, since Cosimo had made the Milanese alliance the very fulcrum of his political system. Ever since Francesco Sforza had become master of Milan, he and Cosimo had guaranteed each other prompt military succor in case of need. The possible failure of the Milanese prop vastly encouraged the anti-Medicean plotters but, fearful of success without arms, they appealed, secretly of course, for aid to Venice, the leading opponent at this time of both Florence and Milan, and also, for good measure, to some small states of the Romagna, notably to Ferrara. Inescapably some months passed before the involved plot could be brought to a head and foreign troops be set in motion across the Apennines toward Tuscany. Their appearance on Tuscan soil was agreed on by the anti-Medicean conspirators as the signal for the local rising.

However, to the complete surprise of the conspirators Piero struck first. Of easy-going temperament he had permitted the stir made by Niccolò Soderini to exhaust itself without interference on his part, in large degree perhaps because he had taken the measure of the impulsive and insubstantial champion of reform. But when, toward the end of August, 1466, he received an urgent message from the friendly ruler of Bologna informing him that hostile troops were moving toward the Florentine border, he acted with prompt and virile resolution. Foreign soldiers crossing into Florentine territory? That transcended the local agitation he had consistently overlooked; that signified war and war, moreover, hatched by treason in the town. It was while residing at Careggi, clamped as usual to his chair by gout, that Piero received the alarming news. Without a moment's hesitation he had himself carried in a litter to the city and taken straight into the presence of the signory to apprise it of the threatening invasion and to urge prompt measures of defense.

It was on August 27 that Piero made his surprise appearance at Florence, thereby challenging the conspirators to come out into the open. They summoned their followers but gave them no orders, they would and they would not. Then, when a few days later, the drawings for office prescribed for September 1 yielded a solid Medicean signory, the half-hearted plot collapsed like a house of cards. The triumph of Piero was complete and, still shaken by the perils he had faced, he used it to crush his adversaries, not, let it be noted, in the bloody manner characteristic of the rest of Italy but in accordance with the milder practices habitual to Florence. A parliament—the old, old trick!—called by the signory took the usual course of conferring all power temporarily on a commission or balìa. Thereupon the balìa, after re-instituting the recently abolished accoppiatori, punished Niccolò Soderini, Agnolo Acciaiuoli, and Diotisalvi Neroni with *confino,* that is, exile, with the further penalty of the confiscation of their property in case they abandoned the town assigned to them as their domicile. To his greater shame

Luca Pitti escaped this sentence. At the height of the crisis he had visited Piero in his sickroom and effected a reconciliation with the unrancorous party leader. Always a flighty person incapable of steering a steady course, Luca, now over seventy years of age, preferred loss of honor to loss of riches coupled with the abandonment of the unfinished Pitti palace which he prized as his enduring monument.

With the domestic rebellion successfully quashed, Piero hoped he could avoid war. It was not to be. The exiles, abandoning their appointed residence, rushed hopefully to Venice and tirelessly importuned the republic of St. Mark and certain rulers of the many petty tyrannies of the Romagna, ever ready for mischief, to join them in order to free Florence from the Medicean pest. They were sufficiently encouraged by the Venetian government to engage as their commander-in-chief the condottiere, Bartolommeo Colleoni, long attached to the service of the republic. Some twenty years later the despicable mercenary had an undeserved immortality conferred on him by the Florentine sculptor, Verrocchio, when, on order of the Venetian state, he created the celebrated equestrian statue of the condottiere which proudly rides the square of the Saints John and Paul in the City of the Lagoons. The hireling soldier received enough support from the states hostile to Florence seriously to threaten the city from his military base in the Romagna. But Florence in the manner of the day hired soldiers in its turn and received the stipulated backing not only from Galeazzo Maria, the new duke of Milan, who had succeeded in getting his rule established on a firm basis, but also from its other ally, the kingdom of Naples. In April, 1468, the rather trifling conflict, usually called from its chief figure the Colleonic War, came to a close in the feckless Italian manner without advantage to either side. The peace treaty, which further raised Piero's mounting prestige, buried the Florentine rebels in oblivion.

Before the crisis precipitated by the Medicean dissidents had been thus happily resolved, before indeed it had even taken definite shape, an honor had been bestowed on the house of Medici of which Piero was understandably proud. In March, 1465, King Louis XI of France issued a diploma which authorized the head of the house of Medici to incorporate three of the lilies of the royal house of Valois in his coat of arms. The Medicean coat of arms in Piero's time was composed of six red balls or *palle* following some fluctuation of their number in the past. The origin and meaning of the balls has occasioned much heraldic debate without arriving at an assured result. The most recent expert pronouncement is to the effect that the origin of the Medici coat of arms is as obscure as that of the Medici family. Be that as it may, dating from the king's patent one of the palle was changed from red (gules) to blue (azure) and on the blue ball appeared stamped in gold the three graciously bestowed French lilies.

Deep as was Piero's satisfaction over the distinction conferred on his house by the king of France, he was too intelligent a man not to have a sense of the risks he was running in submitting to the patronage of the most powerful sovereign of Europe. For that is the position to which Louis XI had attained after the expulsion of the English invaders from France in his father's time and the consolidation of the monarchy that had followed. Already during Cosimo's rule renovated France had begun to cast a steadily lengthening shadow down the Italian peninsula with the result that its many contentious rulers had turned as of one accord toward the French court in the hope of winning its powerful favor. Not only had Cosimo not lagged behind his rivals in this regard but, owing to the ancient commercial association between the Arno city and the French markets, he had fairly outdistanced them all and was publicly hailed by the French king as his most valuable Italian agent. Louis XI, it is true, never went further than to play with the idea of an armed intervention in Italy and, in view of his rooted preference for diplomacy, of which he was a master, over war, which he abhorred, was quite unlikely ever to stumble into the pitfall across the Alps awaiting every ruler rash enough to undertake an invasion. But Louis was not immortal; and who could guarantee that his successor would not take the plunge from which Louis's innate caution persuaded him to hold back? It followed that throughout the rule, first of Piero and afterward of Lorenzo, the French threat hung over Florence like a sword suspended by a thread; and no sooner had Lorenzo departed this life than the slight thread broke and the sword descended with catastrophic consequences for Florence and all Italy.

The chief support of the ailing Piero from the day his rule began was his son Lorenzo. As early as March, 1466, when Lorenzo was only seventeen years old, Piero dispatched him on an embassy to Rome charged with congratulating the new pope, Paul II, on his accession to St. Peter's chair. In a letter, which Piero addressed to Lorenzo during his Roman visit, the father communicated his views on current political issues as freely as if he were dealing with an equal.[1] In simple fact, the precocious youth was already, and remained, the father's alter ego, although he did not on this account fail in respectful filial submission as long as the father lived.

Although in strict point of law Piero was a citizen of the republic of Florence on an exact par with every other citizen, he had inherited from Cosimo a hidden, unofficial control which made him the effective ruler of the city. In the circumstances he could not avoid regarding himself somewhat in the light of a sovereign and, in measure as his children advanced in years, giving the most careful consideration to their politically advantageous disposal in marriage. Accordingly, following established custom, his three daughters were married to members of important Florentine clans, Maria to a Rossi, Bianca to a Pazzi, and Lucrezia (Nannina) to a Rucellai. Calling for much deeper reflection was the marriage of his older son and prospective successor, Lorenzo, and we cannot but agree that both his parents,

[1] For this letter see William Roscoe, *The Life of Lorenzo de' Medici*, Appendix VIII.

intimately tied up as they were with Florentine burgherdom, must have felt a strong pull in favor of a bride from their own class.

But there were considerations not to be overlooked that told against the choice of a local bride. They sprang from the distinct, if officially unadmitted, elevation above their fellow citizens to which the Medici had attained. While not a definitely sovereign family, they were yet sufficiently sovereign not to regard the other Florentine families as any longer their equals, especially when it came to the question of the desirable consort for the heir apparent. Consequently, Piero and Lucrezia were moved to weigh the advantage of a foreign connection and were encouraged to continue their search by the hope of forging an alliance capable of strengthening the Florentine state within the Italian power situation. Their choice fell on a girl of the great Roman family of the Orsini, Clarice by name. The Orsini, an ancient, many-branched feudal clan, were famous for the production of the two outstanding specialties of the fifteenth century soil of Italy, cardinals and condottieri. It was the condottiere, Jacopo, father of Clarice, who with the full knowledge and consent of his brother, the cardinal, signed the contract that bound his daughter in marriage to Lorenzo de' Medici.

Interesting evidence that Piero and Lucrezia, in thus breaking into the highest and oldest aristocratic circles of Italy clung to the caution of their commercial forebears is furnished by the fact that before they clinched the Orsini bargain, Lucrezia made a journey to Rome for the express purpose of having a look at her prospective daughter-in-law. The inspection, politely disguised as a visit to her brother, who served as the head of the Roman branch of the Medici bank, took place in the spring of 1467 and resulted so happily that the contract, indispensable preliminary to marriage, speedily followed. In 1469, Clarice, attended by a suitable escort, came to Florence, and on June 4 of that year she and Lorenzo were joined in wedlock amidst a display so extravagant that we might be tempted to set it down as evidence of the vulgar, new-rich character of the upstart Medici, were it not that a show of material riches coupled with a vast heap of senseless luxury constituted one of the less attractive features of Italian society from the Alps to the strait of Messina during the lauded and often distinctly overlauded Renaissance.

Piero was too stricken to participate actively in the nuptial gaieties of Lorenzo and Clarice. Six months later, on December 2, 1469, he came to the end of his heroically borne sufferings. He was buried in the sacristy of San Lorenzo, where three years later, a magnificent porphyry sarcophagus wrought by the master hand of Verrocchio received his and his brother Giovanni's mortal remains.

VIII

THE RULE OF LORENZO THROUGH
THE PAZZI CONSPIRACY

NOTHING could have been simpler and smoother than the accession of young Lorenzo to the unofficial authority of his father. A few years later, in 1472, he briefly reviewed the events of his life up to that date in *Ricordi*,[1] which recount his accession in the following terms: "On the second day after my father's death, although I, Lorenzo, was only twenty-one years old, the leading men of the city and state came to my house to condole with me and at the same time to request that I assume charge of the city and state as my father and grandfather had done before me. Owing to my youth, I accepted the responsibility with reluctance and solely in the interest of our friends and their fortunes, since at Florence one lives insecurely without the control of the state."

The head and spokesman of the visiting delegation was Tommaso Soderini, brother of that Niccolò, who, only a few years before, had launched a rebellion against Piero. So genuinely was Tommaso attached to Piero that he fell under no suspicion in

---

[1] Published as Appendix XII by Roscoe, *Lorenzo de' Medici*.

connection with his brother's defection and conspicuously re-
warded Piero for his trust in him by instigating the demonstration which was tantamount to the public proclamation of the
succession of Piero's son. The most interesting detail of Lorenzo's
review of the incident, in reality a spicy and revealing political
tidbit, is his indirect explanation as to why there was a Medicean
party. According to this confession, the Mediceans were an association of propertied citizens who held together in order to keep
taxation in their hands and not to let it pass into the control of
their opponents.

On taking power Lorenzo effected no change of system.
While becoming the third under-cover ruler of the city, like
his two predecessors he respected the existing constitution with
its appearance of republican freedom. Holding no regular office,
he had no official title. The address of *Il Magnifico*, which gained
general currency and with which he figures in the pageant of
history, was a simple courtesy title freely conceded in that age
to any person of elevated station.

Born on January 1, 1449, and of an open and eager disposition
from earliest boyhood, Lorenzo, in distinction from his father
and grandfather, received a purely humanistic education tem-
pered by continued immersion in the Catholic faith and practices. The new learning, to which he took as a duck to water,
was at this time sweeping onward to its culmination. Combined
with his love of out-of-doors and sport, it shaped him into the
new social type the age was engaged in hatching, the gentleman,
whose ideal portrait Baldassare Castiglione was later to draw in
his famous *Il Cortigiano*. There was therefore no longer as much
as a trace of the merchant caution and sobriety of Cosimo and
Piero about him, for he had become a spirit, who, liberated from
class trammels, roamed freely through all the realms of thought
and conduct. An unavoidable consequence was an impatience
he developed with the dull details of business and accounts for
a decline that set in before long in the fortunes of the family
bank. What, everything considered, was the most striking single

characteristic of the new lord of Florence, was the harmonious fusion of his many gifts, whereby he appeared to his contemporaries, and continues to appear to us, as an outstanding representative of the culminating Renaissance.

In respect of his physical appearance nature had been distinctly less lavish in endowing him. While he boasted a vigorous frame admirably adapted to the games that were his delight, he was almost repulsively ugly, with sallow complexion, myopic vision, and a flat, spreading nose. As though these drawbacks did not suffice, he was in addition afflicted with a high-pitched voice and almost completely deprived of the sense of smell. In a work,[1] wherein a highly competent authority on heredity has made a thorough examination of the physical characteristics of every member of the Medici clan, it is contended that Lorenzo's flattened nose was an inheritance from his mother's family and that its being broken at the base accounted for the harsh voice and the lack of smell. This same authority is particularly explicit on the subject of the family malady of gout. It must have been latent in Lorenzo from birth, for it commenced to plague him in his middle twenties and, after sending him throughout his last decade on a round of visits among the Tuscan baths in the hope of relief, killed him at the early age of forty-three.

In sharp contrast, Lorenzo's brother, Giuliano, who was four years his junior, was a youth of striking beauty and abounding health. Nor did he yield to Lorenzo in his love of games and his delight in the company of scholars and artists. Struck down by the Pazzi conspiracy at the age of twenty-three, he did not live to realize his promise. By universal testimony he was an alert and amiable young man, who, living in intimate association with his older brother, never for a moment challenged that brother's exclusive political control.

The early years of Lorenzo were relatively uneventful, insofar at least as happenings of great and disturbing political import are concerned. He adhered to the foreign policy which went

[1] Gaetano Pieraccini, *La Stirpe dei Medici di Cafaggiolo.* 3 vols. Firenze, 1925.

back to his grandfather and aimed at maintaining the peace of
the peninsula by an alliance with the duchy of Milan and the
kingdom of Naples. This arrangement had recently proved its
worth by bringing the Colleonic War to a successful termina-
tion, thereby convincing Lorenzo that it adequately served the
purpose for which it was created. Quiet therefore reigned along
the Tuscan borders, and for two years after his accession also
within the borders of the state, when it was broken by a most
distressing episode. It bears the name of Volterra and requires for
its understanding a knowledge of the relationship of Florence to
the once independent communes which had been brought into
gradual subjection in the course of the consolidation of the
Florentine state.

In reducing the Tuscan communities to submission the practice of Florence had been to employ a prudent mixture of dependence and independence. The annexed town (or townlet)
accepted from Florence its two leading officials, the podestà, who
acted as chief executive, and the capitano, who commanded a
small occupying force usually established in a stronghold, called
cassero, incorporated in the fortifications. Under these two representatives of the ruling power the local government was permitted to retain enough liberty in home affairs to flatter the
town pride. In the year 1471 a dispute arose between the local
government of Volterra and a company of capitalists, among
them some Florentines, over the exploitation of certain alum
mines recently discovered in Volterran territory. The turn taken
by this dispute led to an event which has left a serious blot on
Lorenzo's reputation.

Alum was an astringent mineral indispensable in the process-
ing of wool and had originally been derived from Asia Minor.
Shortly after the middle of the fifteenth century a rich deposit
of the mineral had been discovered at Tolfa in the papal states,
and its exploitation, which proved highly profitable, had been
contractually accorded by the pope to the Medici firm. When,
therefore, another alum bed was uncovered south of Volterra, a

company was quickly formed which undertook its exploitation on the strength of a contract with the town government. The new bed was of inferior quality and proved in the end to be unprofitable. However, in 1471, when the contract was drawn up, this was not yet known and the misinformed inhabitants of Volterra demonstrated so vigorously against their municipal government on the charge that the agreement did not sufficiently protect the interest of the commune that the document was withdrawn and the mines closed by municipal action until a new contract should be signed.

At this point the suzerain power, Florence, intervened in behalf of the exploiting company and ordered the Volterran government to release the mines. The order produced a riot culminating in an assault on the Florentine podestà, who was obliged to seek safety in flight. To Lorenzo's mind, as to the mind of the whole Florentine population, the rising was rebellion and needed to be sternly dealt with. Not improbably, the issue could have been quickly settled by resort to negotiation. But because the Florentines were nervous over their imperfect hold on the conquered towns, which without exception continued to nurse the dream of independence, and certainly also because Lorenzo was young and untried, he chose to appeal to force. The usual mercenary army was assembled and dispatched against the town, high-planted on one of the barren hills that line the western coast of Tuscany.

It did not require a long siege to persuade the town to surrender on terms that secured the inhabitants in life and goods. But when, on June 17, 1472, the Florentine condottiere, Federigo of Montefeltro, rode into the town at the head of his mercenaries, a terrible thing happened. Like all mercenaries, those under Federigo lived on pay supplemented by looting and robbery. The sight of the helpless population so excited their cupidity that they broke rank and put the town to a devastating sack. Conceding that the monstrous event is referable, in the main, to the hideous military system of the period, we cannot entirely absolve Lorenzo from responsibility, for it was he, who, rejecting the idea of an amicable settlement and resolved to make an example of Volterra, had decided for war. We cannot doubt his subsequent regret at his hasty decision, since, following the event, he did what he could, and it was little enough, to relieve the misery and degradation the sack had brought on the town.

The peace enjoyed by Italy following Lorenzo's coming to power was broken by the pope. It was in 1471, on the death of Paul II, that the cardinals raised to the papal throne a Franciscan friar, offspring of hardy Ligurian fisherfolk, who took the title of Sixtus IV. It was in no way unusual that he should have begun his reign by indulging in the practice of nepotism, which the church had from the early Middle Ages stigmatized as a sin and which consisted in loading nephews and relatives with ecclesiastical benefits. Almost his first act following his elevation was to raise two of his nephews, Giuliano della Rovere, who bore his own family name, and Pietro Riario, the son of his sister married to a Riario, to a cardinalate. He then continued to heap ecclesiastical honors on Pietro especially, until it seemed that all the riches of the church were to be dropped into his lap. Cardinal Riario, thus favored, developed an insane passion for luxury and a mad self-indulgence, from the combined effect of which he died at an early age in 1474. Thereupon Sixtus drew from the obscurity of a minor clerkship a younger brother of Pietro, Girolamo by name, and proceeded to push him upward at the same dizzy pace as he had pushed his deceased brother with the distinction that he endowed Girolamo with secular, not ecclesiastical honors.

And here we must pause to have a look at the relation of the pope to the numerous distinct territories making up the State of the Church. These territories—the country around Rome identical with ancient Latium, Umbria, the Marshes of Ancona, and the Romagna—had never been brought into effective papal subjection. Petty tyrants, whom the supreme pontiff had not proved strong enough to remove, had established themselves in the towns and were left in possession in return for the formal acknowledgment of the papal supremacy coupled with the payment of a small tribute. Of course the Renaissance popes chafed under this humiliating situation, but until Sixtus came to power failed to make a serious effort to remedy it. And when Sixtus did brace himself to the undertaking, being the nepotistic pope he was, he could think of no better way to proceed than to replace as many petty tyrants as he could unseat or buy off with one or another of his nephews, more particularly with the aforementioned, much loved but wholly despicable Girolamo. In 1474 he scored his first success in the new policy by satisfying the claimant to the town of Imola with the down-payment of forty thousand ducats and by then handing Imola over to Girolamo.

The papal move put an end to the good terms on which Sixtus IV and Lorenzo had hitherto lived. Imola lay in the Romagna eastward of the Tuscan Apennines and together with half a dozen similar lordships formed a protective belt around the Florentine state. If it was the purpose of the reigning pope to gain direct control of these small dominions, thus consolidating the papal possessions, Florence had reason for alarm, for it bordered on the south, east, and north on the hitherto weak and militarily inoffensive papal state. Moreover, should the plan of Sixtus be crowned with success, the four states, Venice, Milan, Florence, Naples, making up what for some decades past had figured as the dominant powers of Italy, would be augmented by a fifth state, and this fifth state would be a potential threat to all the others but, especially, owing to its geographical position, to adjoining Tuscany. Power situations are notoriously productive of fear and Lorenzo, taking alarmed note of the pope's new territorial policy, resolved to balk it but, in order not needlessly to offend Sixtus IV, to move as invisibly and subterraneanly as possible.

On proceeding with his cherished recovery plan the pope was not long in learning that the local resistances he encountered in the Romagna and in Umbria were secretly encouraged by Lorenzo, who, in the light of these disclosures, revealed himself as a treacherous enemy. In November, 1474, Lorenzo made matters worse by a radical shift in foreign policy. He abandoned the well-tried triple alliance of Florence-Milan-Naples and replaced it with an agreement with Milan and Venice, which states, bordering, like Florence, on the territories of the church, were hardly less disturbed than himself by the papal program of consolidation. Sixtus promptly countered by teaming up with Naples, thus dividing Italy into two mutually suspicious, hostile leagues. While the association of the three northern powers was decidedly stronger than that of the two southern ones, there was the countervailing fact of the pope's inflammable temper and his power as head of the church to do his enemies grievous ecclesiastical despite. Savagely driven to square accounts, he raised a bitter Florentine enemy of Lorenzo to the archbishopric of Pisa. The appointee was a member of the Salviati family, Francesco by name, and he was elevated to the Pisan dignity, in spite of an earlier solemn undertaking on the part of the pope not to appoint any prelates to Tuscan sees without previous consultation with the Florentine government. The relations between the head of the church and the ruler of Florence were steadily becoming increasingly strained, when there befell an event in Milan, the moral implications of which gravely deepened the existing division.

On December 26, 1476, three Milanese youths waylaid Duke Galeazzo Maria as he was entering the church of St. Stephen and stabbed him to death. In the trial that followed it was revealed that they had been incited to the deed by their humanist teacher, Cola Montano, who had systematically inflamed their imaginations with the encomiums lavished by certain classical authors on the practice of tyrannicide. Since the murdered duke was one of the most infamous representatives of the current tyrant type, it is not likely that a single tear was shed over his violent exit from the world. Nonetheless, it had consequences of the gravest import. For one thing it brought political confusion to Milan, owing to the fact that the duke's heir was a three-year-old boy and that a regency had to be appointed to function in his name. While this office was assigned to the boy's mother, the boy's four lusty and ambitious uncles, brothers of the late duke, claimed it for themselves with the result that Milan, temporarily at least, ceased to count as a great power and that Lorenzo, the ally of Milan, was proportionately enfeebled. Another consequence of the murder was the wide and encouraging currency it gave to the pagan doctrine of tyrannicide. It is not unlikely, although it cannot be proved, that it was the Milanese instance which first directed the thought of the most venomous enemies of the Medici to their removal by the classically exalted instrumentality of murder.

The central figure of the resulting plot was without question Girolamo Riario, who, though now in unchallenged possession of Imola, nursed in his bosom a savage resentment against Lorenzo because of his continued secret machinations in the Romagna. At Rome, under the pope's wing, where he spent much of his time, he encountered another young man animated with a similar unreasoning hatred of Lorenzo and the whole Medici family. This was Francesco Pazzi, nephew of old Jacopo Pazzi, chief of one of the oldest Florentine families and head of a bank, which was in sharp competition with the rival institution of the Medici. Francesco was in charge of the Roman branch of the Pazzi bank and had recently scored a considerable triumph by persuading Sixtus IV to transfer the invaluable papal account from the Medici firm to that of the Pazzi.

The two impassioned young men mutually incited each other to the deed and presently drew Francesco Salviati into their counsels. Appointed archbishop of Pisa by the pope, he was for three years forcibly hindered by the angered Lorenzo from taking possession of his post; and even after Lorenzo had at last relented, the archbishop's rage and rancor continued to burn at fever heat. The next logical step before the plotters was to win over the pope, a measure which, in view of the now open cleavage between him and Lorenzo, seemed easy to accomplish. This, however, proved not to be the case, for at the first mention of bloodshed, Sixtus discovered his Christian conscience and drew back in horror. His prolonged siege by the conspirators resulted in a compromise. While hotly declaring in favor of the extinction of the Medici rule as an abomination in the sight of God and man, he refused to give his sanction to the murder of the two brothers who were the living representatives of that rule. He might as well have agreed that they be drowned but not in water! Fully conscious of the ambiguity of the papal position, the cunning plotters quietly went ahead with their plans, convinced that they would not fail to obtain the papal blessing after the event.

It now became necessary to pick a competent military man to head the enterprise and a certain Gian Batista da Montesecco, a mercenary captain in the employ of the lord of Imola, accepted the appointment and continued in charge of the details of the projected murder almost to the moment of action. He then withdrew on being informed that the double slaughter (for the plotters were never in doubt that both brothers would have to be dispatched simultaneously) was set to come off in church during the celebration of mass. As a professional brigand, Montesecco was ready to oblige with murder at a reasonable fee, but, being at the same time a Christian brigand, he refused to work at his trade in church and had, at a late stage of the preparations, to be replaced. However, he did not leave town and was captured after the event. This is distinctly important, since before he was tried and executed he wrote out a circumstantial confession, which is our leading source of information on the plot.[1]

After several hurried, last-minute shifts, it was at last agreed that the double assassination was to take place in the cathedral of Santa Maria del Fiore during the celebration of High Mass

---

[1] Published at the end of the second volume by G. Capponi, *Storia della Repubblica di Firenze*. 2 vols. Firenze, 1875.

on Sunday, April 26, 1478; and since it was a question not only of the removal of Lorenzo and Giuliano but also of the overthrow of their government, an appropriate distribution of roles was made with the leads assigned as follows: two disaffected priests volunteered to replace the over-sensitive soldier Montesecco and to account for Lorenzo; Francesco Pazzi and another young Florentine coxcomb, Bernardo Bandini, took on themselves the responsibility for Giuliano; the archbishop Salviati agreed to seize the palace of the priors and take over the government; and Jacopo dei Pazzi, a wizened old man hardly able any longer to sit a horse, was delegated to mount his war-steed and from his saddle to exhort his fellow citizens to join him in the heartening struggle for the recovery of their lost liberty. Old Jacopo, an avaricious miser of bad repute, had long resisted his nephew Francesco's importunities to take part in the plot. Only after it had ripened to the point where it seemed that it could not fail did he consent to play the role assigned to him and sound the tocsin summoning the people to cast off a hateful yoke.

But where was Girolamo Riario, the original conspirator, and what part in the undertaking was allotted to him? It defines his heroic quality that he preferred not to risk his precious neck; however, in order that the papal family be not unrepresented in a crime of which it was the chief fomenter, he agreed that a young nephew of his and grand-nephew of the pope be drawn into the murder cast in the role of a decoy. Only seventeen years old, this nephew was a living witness that the church was in headlong decay by having already been raised to the dignity of cardinal. Too young as yet to function in this capacity at Rome, he was completing his education at the University of Pisa when the conspirators summoned him to Florence. It was agreed that he should announce himself to the Medici rulers as paying them a visit of respect. This would assure a series of official events, one of which was the solemn mass finally chosen as the occasion for springing the plot. The presence of the young cardinal would make it obligatory for both the Medici hosts to attend. It has been assumed, and is probably correct, that the youth was not informed either of the conspiracy or of the dark implications of the merely representative role assigned to him.

The signal agreed on for the simultaneous assassination of the brothers was the most solemn moment of the service, the elevation of the host; and no sooner, to the tinkling of the mass bell, was the host elevated by the officiating priest standing before the high-altar under Brunelleschi's majestic dome than the murderers leaped upon their victims. Francesco Pazzi and Bernardo Bandini quickly dispatched the young and handsome Giuliano. When he was later laid out for burial, it was discovered that he had poured out his life-blood from twenty-nine gaping wounds. In such blind rage did Francesco Pazzi hack at the prostrate form of his victim that he wounded himself in the thigh so severely that it was only with the greatest difficulty that he made his escape from the scene. The two priests allotted to Lorenzo proved themselves decidedly less expert in the art of murder than the two civilians. On receiving a glancing blow on the shoulder, Lorenzo alertly turned on his assailants and with drawn sword held them at bay until, with the help of friends who rallied to his support, he succeeded in taking refuge in the sacristy. When the vast concourse of worshipers, rocked by the confusion as by an earthquake, had sped away in every direction, the followers of Lorenzo, acting as his bodyguard and humanely shielding him from the view of Giuliano lying in a pool of blood, led him from the desecrated Christian temple to the safety of his home.

While this only half-successful man-hunt was being conducted around the principal altar of one of the great cathedrals of Christendom, the archbishop Salviati and old Jacopo Pazzi attempted to fulfill the respective roles assigned to them. They failed miserably for the reason that both the sitting priors and the Florentine people sided with practical unanimity with their reputed tyrants. On invading the palace with a band of supporters the archbishop and his ruffians were promptly put under arrest; and when old Jacopo, looking for all the world like a caricature of the vanished age of chivalry, rode through the streets hoarsely shouting *Popolo* and *Libertà,* the ancient rallying-cries of the Florentine masses, he had hurled back at him a lusty *Palle, Palle,* to let him know that the Medici had the enthusiastic support of the masses.

Thus, in spite of the murder of Giuliano, the conspiracy had failed, and quiet might have been restored, had it not been for the wild resentment against the plotters that washed over the people like a tidal wave. They became that murderous thing, a mob, which called for blood and would not be denied. Obedient to the raucous summons from the multitude solidly massed in the piazza, the priors tossed the captured minions of the archbishop out of the windows to the pavement much as a keeper might toss meat into a den of hunger-crazed tigers; and finally, they followed up this gesture of appeasement by swinging the archbishop himself with a rope around his neck out of one of the Gothic windows, there to hang in his ornate vestments till he was dead. In another part of the city the mob invaded the Pazzi palace to seize the murderer Francesco, who was lying in bed writhing with his self-inflicted wound, and drag him to the palace of the priors that he might dangle from another mullioned window, a worthy companion figure to the traitorous archbishop.

The hunt for old Jacopo was unsuccessful, for, overcome with panic, he had made off for the hills. But he could not escape his fate. Captured by peasants, he was brought back to the city, cruelly tortured, and hanged. Young Cardinal Riario was saved by the government taking him into its safekeeping. Even the hate-blinded multitude recognized that he was but the dupe of his criminal elders and desisted from its original intention to have his blood. The tumultuous excitement continued for days and even weeks, since the demand for vengeance raged like a fever and insisted that every participant in the crime without exception should be brought to an accounting. The most striking case of the ferocious pursuit of this purpose was furnished by Bernardo Bandini. He had fled with the hot breath of the chase upon his back all the way to distant Constantinople, but, brought back after many months, like all the other culprits, he paid for his crime with his life. In spite of the share in the far-flung plot of individuals of many different political allegiances, to the Florentines the conspiracy was pre-eminently a quarrel between two native families, and the name they gave it of the Pazzi Conspiracy became its accepted historical label.

Although with Lorenzo alive and the whole town fanatically demonstrating its devotion to him, the plot had been defeated, the threat to himself and his state was by no means ended. It may even be said that it still remained to be faced, since the pope, balked of his prey, refused to consider any feature of the revolting drama save the enforced detention at Florence of his grand-nephew and the indignities heaped upon the sacred person of an archbishop. In his wrath he excommunicated Lorenzo, to all appearances for unlawful resistance to murder; and he threatened to put Florence and all Tuscany under interdict if the malefactor be not promptly delivered into his hands. When the city indignantly rejected this demand, the interdict was pronounced and immediately followed by war. Shoulder to shoulder with the pope stood his ally, the king of Naples. Calling on his own allies of Venice and Milan to take their stand at his side, Lorenzo assembled, as for that matter did all the others, the usual mercenary army. By the summer of 1478 all Italy was in arms, with many of the numerous small states joining one or the other of the two major combinations.

Almost at once the war took a turn unfavorable to Florence and Lorenzo. The mercenaries proved as unreliable as they had always been, and his allies gave him insufficient support. Venice was at the time engaged in a war with the Turks which was understandably felt to be more directly pressing than the Florentine call for help; and Milan was so disturbed by the continuing conflict between the regent-mother of the boy-duke and her intriguing brothers-in-law that its government was effectively paralyzed.

In the circumstances King Ferrante of Naples and Sixtus IV were able to take the offensive by invading Tuscany and might quickly have overwhelmed Lorenzo if their warfare had not been under the same mercenary curse as that of their opponent. Even so, they came within an ace of destroying him. In the autumn of the second campaign, fought in 1479, King Ferrante's son, Alfonso, duke of Calabria, launched a surprise attack against the Florentine army encamped at Poggio Imperiale in the Elsa valley and drove it in headlong flight toward Florence. Not till the panic-stricken fugitives had reached San Casciano, some eight miles from the Tuscan capital, could they be regathered into the semblance of a fighting force. Had the duke of Calabria undauntedly pushed on, he would almost certainly have held Florence at his mercy. But such boldness was not in the military style of the day. Instead of pressing his advantage, the duke let himself be stopped by the small blockading town of Colle and, on November 24, on the approach of winter, proposed the usual seasonal truce, which the Florentines eagerly accepted.

When, on the signing of the truce, Lorenzo examined the situation, he found it to be desperate. The war had been fought throughout on Tuscan soil and been attended by the familiar destruction of crops and plunder of the population. With an exhausted treasury and with famine and famine's twin brother, pestilence, stalking through the land, peace had become an imperative necessity. But how win it from the vengeful pope save by unconditional surrender? Happily the pope's fighting arm was the king of Naples and the prospect beckoned that the king might not prove equally implacable. In Lorenzo's considered view it was contrary to the interest of the southern kingdom to let the pope sweep the boards and wax too powerful. So sure was he of his ground that he was persuaded he could make King

Ferrante see the error of his ways, if only he might meet him face to face. But how bring that about, except by the hazardous and unexampled step of taking ship and sailing boldly over the waters to knock as a petitioner at the door of the king's palace?

It was a fortunate circumstance that the troublesome Milanese situation had recently become clarified by one of the contentious uncles of the boy-duke winning the right of serving as sole regent. This was Lodovico Sforza who, with a sympathetic understanding for Lorenzo's evil plight, now approached Ferrante of Naples and was informed that the king would not decline to hear the Florentine ruler personally plead his cause. The news relayed to Lorenzo fixed his wavering purpose. To be sure, it offered no assurance of any sort and might be no more than a ruse to get him into his enemy's power; but since there was no other way out of his crushing predicament, he resolved to take the chance. Detractors might afterward declare, and of course did not fail to do so, that he was prompted by nothing better than the desire to save himself and his rule, but no amount of belittlement can obscure the fact that he was mainly concerned to save his country. At any rate that such was the case was the spontaneous judgment of his fellow citizens when they learned that on nightfall of a day in early December he had secretly left the city and on the coast below Pisa had taken ship for the bay of Naples. No Florentine doubted that to thus put himself into the hands of a king practiced in every treachery was an act of patriotic self-sacrifice and no fair-minded historian has ever rated it other than as a deed of the highest moral courage.

Lorenzo was not disappointed by the reception accorded him on his arrival at Naples. But he trod no path of roses, since the king and, more especially, his son, the duke of Calabria, had no thought of letting Florence escape without paying some of the usual penalties of defeat. For two months Lorenzo with cogent eloquence and ever gracious manners argued the terms of peace with his hosts, until in February, 1480, a treaty had taken shape.

By its articles Florence was obliged to pay a considerable money indemnity and accept some not inconsiderable rectifications of territory, but only an intemperate critic would aver that, on returning home, Lorenzo had not brought back peace with honor. His countrymen accordingly overflowed with gratitude and the government of the priors, to which the document was submitted for approval, formally and swiftly sanctioned it.

The acceptance, signifying the official end of the war, took place on March 25, which, as it chanced, was the very day on which Pope Sixtus IV added his own name to the treaty. Gravely offended by the unfaithfulness of his ally of Naples in agreeing to a separate peace, he could hit on no effective measure of undoing it, owing to his inability to continue the struggle by himself. However, the cessation of war did not remove the ecclesiastical penalties imposed by him before the war had started: Lorenzo's excommunication and the interdict, the effect of which had been to darken every altar in Tuscany. Nor is it likely that the penalties would have been lifted at an early date, had not the hidden rulers of the universe in their ever capricious way now come to Lorenzo's aid.

On a hot August day of this same year of 1480 a Turkish flotilla made a sudden descent on the Neapolitan harbor-town of Otranto and captured it. At this first Moslem penetration of Italian soil an apprehensive tremor shook the peninsula throughout its length. The duke of Calabria with the Neapolitan army had lingered on in Tuscany in the hope of extorting territorial advantages from Lorenzo beyond the strict letter of the treaty. The blow that fell at Otranto obliged him to hurry home with all possible speed. The following year he succeeded in recapturing Otranto, a triumph which stands out as the single memorable achievement of his undistinguished career. Although we are only indirectly concerned with the history of Italy, it is fitting and even imperative that so important an event as the repulse of the Turks and the attendant liberation of the peninsula be here recorded. For Lorenzo the Otranto episode proved a pure cause of rejoicing, for it had forced the Neapolitan army and its treacherous general to abandon Tuscany.

Nor was this the only advantage accruing to Lorenzo from the alarming descent of the Turks. In the face of the Moslem invasion of Italy Sixtus IV had recalled to his mind his responsibilities as shepherd of the Christian flock. Fervently, for he was a passionate man, he urged all Italians to join hearts and hands in resisting the infidels, and with exhortations of unity on his lips, he could no longer with any show of decency pursue his private grudge against Lorenzo. He let himself be drawn into negotiations which, before the year was over, ended in a formal act of reconciliation. Enthroned before the middle door of St. Peter's church in purple robes and with the papal tiara on his head, Sixtus received a body of Florentine commissioners and by touching each in turn with his staff cleansed them, and by implication the whole Florentine population including Lorenzo, of the heretical taint he had laid upon them. Thus at long last was brought to rest the bitter conflict between Sixtus IV and Lorenzo de' Medici.

IX

THE RULE OF LORENZO FROM THE
PAZZI CONSPIRACY TO HIS DEATH

FROM the Pazzi Conspiracy and the subsequent war Lorenzo had escaped as from an engulfing shipwreck, and when, from the safe shore, he looked out over the retreating waters, he did not content himself with laying the blame for his agonizing experience on the senseless elements. He, too, had been at fault, and the core and substance of his error had been his departure from the peace policy inaugurated by his grandfather, continued by his father, and adopted on his accession by himself. Out of fear of the consequences for his own state he had interfered with the plan of the pope to convert his many loosely held territories into an effective State of the Church; and in pursuit of this purpose he had abandoned the triple alliance of Milan, Naples, and Florence, which was a league of peace, for the triple alliance of Milan, Venice, and Florence with the offensive implications deriving from its purpose to thwart the pope's ambition.

Originally, and through the ages in every essential respect, the pope, as head of the Christian church, was a spiritual ruler.

But as early as the eighth century he had become also a temporal ruler and in this capacity had gradually brought under his scepter an impressive mass of dependencies spread over central and north-central Italy. Unfortunately for him, he had not been able to prevent, on the one hand, the feudal magnates of his dominion, and, on the other hand, the developing towns from making themselves substantially independent, even though formally they continued to acknowledge his suzerainty. When the movement toward political consolidation became general in Italy and culminated in the rise of the four leading states of Venice, Milan, Florence, and Naples, it was understandable that the pope should have wished to raise himself to a temporal level with them as a fifth Italian power. However, not till the Great Schism had been overcome in the first half of the fifteenth century was it possible even seriously to ponder the problem, while effectively to attack it proved impossible, owing to the elective, and therefore discontinuous, character of the papacy coupled with its lack of military power.

It was the continuing temporal weakness of the papacy that had brought Pope Sixtus IV around to the idea of strengthening his authority by establishing his relatives in the papal territories; and, as we are aware, he inaugurated the new policy by setting up his nephew, Girolamo Riario, at Imola. The aggrandizing of relatives, more particularly nephews, out of the resources of the church had for ages been so common a papal practice that its adoption by Sixtus did not send as much as a ripple of moral indignation through the land. Besides, with Italian civilization entering, in the time of Sixtus, on its Renaissance phase, the Roman court had become steeped in the new worldliness which had fanned out until it had penetrated society from top to bottom. It is too well known to require elaboration that the popes of the period surrounded themselves with a brilliant court and prided themselves on the role they played as patrons of literature and art. The situation is here recalled to the sole end of bringing out that in the eyes of the Italian contemporaries of Sixtus there was nothing notably improper in his planting his nephew at Imola and in proposing to give the papal territories a more effective organization.

It should therefore be clearly understood that when Lorenzo de' Medici undertook to cross the pope's territorial plans, being himself, like Sixtus, a man of the Renaissance, he had been motivated not by religious but exclusively by secular considerations. His mistake had been to underestimate the retaliatory power of the pope and overestimate the support he would be given by his allies, Venice and Milan; and the consequence had been his catastrophic defeat. Then, at the darkest point of his career he proved his moral and mental flexibility by completely reversing himself. Not only did he renounce his opposition to the pope in respect of the papal territories but he gave up the league with Venice and Milan formed to foil the pope and returned to the older, time-tested alliance, with Milan and Naples. He even undertook to expand the revived triple into a quintuple alliance by the inclusion of Venice and the pope, although this enlargement to his keen regret was never realized. Nonetheless, he busied himself unremittingly with mediating among the ever contentious Italian states, and by his consistent striving for peace fully merited the fame he enjoyed at his death of having been the leading promoter in his day of peninsular unity.

While we may agree that in this second period of his rule Lorenzo played the part of pacifier from an intelligent appreciation of the material and cultural benefits conferred by peace, he had also another reason which needs to be carefully set forth. Already in the days of his grandfather and father the king of France had occasionally been moved to take a distant hand in the Italian political game and in the hope and expectation of private advantage had repeatedly been urged by one and another of the irresponsible Italian rulers to cross the Alps at the head of an army. But neither Charles VII nor his son, Louis XI, absorbed as they both were with the consolidation of the royal power, seriously considered the proposal. Just the same, a French threat had taken shape and hung all but visibly suspended over the peninsula. From the very beginning of his rule the watchful Lorenzo had reckoned with it in his assessment of the general situation. Then, with the death in 1483 of the wary Louis XI, whom his none too loving subjects called "the Spider," and the accession to the throne of the youthful Charles VIII, the threat gained depth and substance from the ambitious character of the new ruler coupled with his acquisition of a claim to the kingdom of Naples.

In this latter connection let us recall that somewhat past the middle of the thirteenth century Charles of Anjou, brother of the then king of France, Louis IX, had succeeded in replacing King Manfred of the German house of Hohenstaufen as monarch of Sicily. His descendants had continued to rule in mainland Naples (but not in the island of Sicily) until driven from their kingdom after something less than two hundred years by the Spanish house of Aragon. Their expulsion notwithstanding, the Angevins continued to lay claim to Naples, and when, in 1481, the last Angevin died, his claim was transmitted to the ruling house of France, the house of Valois. Promptly following his accession young King Charles VIII was incited by his flattering courtiers to keep ever before him the plan of expelling the Aragonese occupant of Naples as a usurper and of appropriating the kingdom to himself on the strength of what the courtiers represented to him as his indefeasible right.

In addition to the Neapolitan claim another French connection with the Italian situation fell with a certain, though less telling, weight into the scales. In the days of the Visconti rule of Milan the duke of Orléans, head of a younger line of the house of Valois, had married a Visconti princess with the result that her French descendants claimed title to Milan and stigmatized the actual holders of the Milanese duchy, that is, the rude condottiere, Sforza, and his descendants as unqualified usurpers. Constantly reminded by the interested court circles of the Neapolitan enterprise, King Charles could also at his pleasure make the claim of his living relative, the duke of Orléans, his own and by the merger of both claims see Italy in the rosy light of a country where two considerable inheritances were waiting to be picked up by him at the slight inconvenience of an armed expedition across the Alps.

It was the alarming prospect of a French descent on Italy that constituted the mainspring of the unceasing effort on the part of Lorenzo in behalf of peace. In his opinion nothing short of the united front of the five leading Italian states would serve to stave off a French intervention. His arguments proved without avail among rulers whose petty differences so feverishly stirred their blood that they simply could not be persuaded to renounce them. Out of the abundant evidence of the persistence of this unhappy frame of mind we shall content ourselves with presenting two instances. From 1482 to 1484, which were the last years of his reign, the bellicose Sixtus IV joined with Venice in a war against Ferrara for the openly announced purpose of partitioning it between them. Their action brought the triple alliance of Milan, Naples, and Florence into the field in support of Ferrara and the crude scheme was defeated. However, throughout the Ferrarese war Italy was in tumult. And hardly had this particular disturbance been quieted, when the successor of Sixtus IV, Pope Innocent VIII, fell out (1485) with King Ferrante of Naples and continued in open or concealed war with him for almost seven years.

Clearly, in spite of the danger looming from across the Alps, there was no peace in Italy in Lorenzo's day. There was even a short war of his own, which, though he regretted, he saw no way to escape. It concerned the fortress of Sarzana, northward of Florence along the Ligurian coast. In the year 1468 his father, Piero, had gained title to Sarzana by purchase from a powerful Genoese family, the Fregosi. But, a treacherous clan, they had taken advantage of Lorenzo's embarrassments during the disastrous war which followed the Pazzi Conspiracy to regain possession of Sarzana. Although committed to a policy of peace, the Magnificent was not for peace at any price. Nor could he afford to be in view of the patriotic ardor of the Florentines, whose clamorously voiced demand was that, if their ruler lacked the power to enlarge their state, he must at least maintain its undiminished integrity. Proceeding with the greatest caution, for he wished at all costs to avoid a general conflagration, he took advantage of a favorable opportunity and in June, 1487, recaptured Sarzana after a short siege. His personal presence during the final headlong storming of the citadel by his troops had the happy effect of exhibiting him to his people as the active guardian of their rights and reputation.

However, when all the circumstances are considered, a certain ambiguity must be admitted to have invested Lorenzo's peace policy, owing to the character of his relations with the French king. Let us agree that he lived in genuine dread of his Gallic neighbor and never ceased urging his Italian fellow rulers to stand together in order to seal up every avenue of penetration into the peninsula. But while thus consistently hostile to the French king on sound political grounds, he was obliged for reasons of an economic nature to hover uninterruptedly as a suitor about the steps of his throne. France was still, as it had been from before the distant days of Dante, a leading market for Florentine woolen products. More recently some specialties of the Florentine silk looms had also gained favor in French circles, especially among the upper classes. In a certain sense Florence had flourished materially in the past, and was still flourishing in the present, on the bounty of France and the benefits conferred by that country were reflected in the extraordinary popularity it enjoyed on the Arno. On taking over the rule of the city the prudent first representative of the house of Medici had carefully nursed the French economic tie together with the sentiment of devotion it excited among his countrymen; and in 1465, Cosimo's successor, Piero, had achieved the high distinction of being, as it were, adopted into the royal family by the privilege conferred by Louis XI of incorporating three French lilies in his coat of arms.

To the reasons of a public nature for cultivating close relations with France was added the special and private reason of the family bank. But as the far-ranging interests of the bank, which, as from the beginning, was also a trading company, required good relations with every country in which one of its branches operated, it will be desirable for us to extend our vision at this point to cover the total story of the complex institution in Lorenzo's day. We have already noted that it achieved its greatest prosperity under Cosimo and Piero and that it started visibly downhill under Lorenzo. We have also indicated that it was Lorenzo's lack of interest in business and his insufficient commercial training that explains the turning of the tide. A flaw of related nature was his failure adequately to control his agents, although it is but fair to insist that the concession to his foreign representatives of a large measure of independence was unavoidable, owing to their great distance from the parent house and the often dangerous delay this imposed on the exchange of advice.

The heavy blow struck Lorenzo by the failure of the Medici bank at Bruges in the Netherlands was directly attributable to one of these unreliable representatives. He was Tommaso Portinari, descendant of a Florentine family of great distinction as far back as Dante's day. Lovers of the poet will at once recall that the shadowy Beatrice, to whom he dedicated a lifelong service, bore the Portinari name. By many years of clerk-service at Bruges, Tommaso had at last risen to the post of command. His financial talents, which were considerable, led him astray by persuading him that he might considerably swell his profits by hazardous political, instead of safe, commercial loans. In this frame of mind he backed Duke Charles of Burgundy, to whom his contemporaries gave the by-name of Charles the Rash, in his mad plan to build up a powerful independent state between France and Germany. When he crowned his fast declining fortunes by getting himself killed in battle against the Swiss in

1477, Portinari's immense investment in the reckless adventurer became a total loss.

Tommaso Portinari seems to have exercised some influence over the decisions of the manager of the neighboring branch at London. Whether he did or not, the London representative adopted Portinari's policy of extending himself too freely in political loans. It was the time in England of the civil war called the War of the Roses, and on the London branch supporting King Edward IV with huge subsidies, it found itself before long with only valueless paper on its hands. It is certain that Lorenzo had to come to the rescue at both London and Bruges with the dispatch of large amounts of gold florins from Florence. Then, in order to avoid further losses, he liquidated both institutions during the heavy seas in which he floundered at the time of the Pazzi Conspiracy.

The precise situation at London and Bruges, as indeed at every other branch bank, has remained involved in considerable uncertainty. This is particularly true of the branch at Lyons, which was not established till 1466, when it expanded rapidly under the sunshine of Louis XI's favor. However, for no other reason, so far at least as available documents serve to indicate, than the incompetent management of the head of the branch at Lyons, Lionetto de' Rossi, such difficulties arose that after a few years Lorenzo was obliged to re-organize the firm after pocketing a considerable loss. Following a period of prosperity ascribable to the continued support of the French king, a second crisis ensued at Lyons on the king's death in 1483. In one of those irrational panics to which depositors have always been prone, they started a run on the bank which led to another heavy loss for Lorenzo followed by another expensive re-organization. While the repeated failures here recorded seem to have been due in the main to the incompetence of the branch managers, other factors, which escape precise definition, figured in the collapse. Among them, it is highly probable, a Europe-wide economic and financial depression played a not negligible role.

The successive crises at London, Bruges, and Lyons could not be concealed in a world banking center like Florence nor could a heap of irresponsible gossip be averted as to how Lorenzo found the means to meet the several emergencies. His enemies, unable to speak their minds freely in public, intrusted the suspicions they entertained to diaries which are still extant and have in part been published. With a varying degree of venom they asserted that, in order to escape from his financial jam, the Magnificent had had recourse to the public funds. While this is a charge which may under no circumstances be overlooked, an objective and fair-minded inquiry demands that it be examined in close connection with the total issue of the finances of the Florentine republic in Lorenzo's day.

There can be no doubt that, beginning with Cosimo, the private finances of the ruling family became variously entangled with those of the state. This may at first have been an advantage for the state, since Cosimo, the prosperous banker, was able to help out with advances from his private funds whenever the need arose. In addition to such direct financial aid he, and Piero after him, performed certain unremunerated public services as, for instance, the entertainment in their palace and at their own expense of high-placed official visitors. By Lorenzo's time the situation had undergone a change in several not unimportant respects. The declining bank was much less able to come to the help of the state in periods of stress and the third ruler of the house had assumed so much more visibly and magnificently the headship of the state that his expenses in this role had been vastly increased. He entertained visiting princes and their suites in the great palace in the via Larga often for many days and the display characteristic of this age of upstarts required him to practice a prodigal hospitality. Neither for this nor for the embassies he dispatched to the courts of his fellow rulers did he receive compensation; and if, on discovering that the inherited Fortunatus purse no longer automatically dropped gold florins into his palm, he argued that he had impoverished himself in the service of the state, he was not entirely in the wrong.

His ambiguous situation arose from the fact that, since his tyranny was unofficial, there could be no accounting between him and the government and that, if he dipped his hands into the public treasury, he was, regardless of his private convictions, formally guilty of theft. And the guilt would be greater, much greater, in case, as his enemies charged, he appropriated public funds to meet the private losses suffered through the failure of the branches of the family enterprise at London, Bruges, and Lyons. That he committed this grave malfeasance, and to what extent, will always remain a matter of conjecture, but that there were irregularities due, in the main, to his unclarified official position is, to put it mildly, not improbable. His whispering enemies specifically charged him with appropriations from two public funds of outstanding importance. One was the public debt (*Il Monte*), the other a dower fund for girls called *Il Monte delle Doti*. Since, however, they were not able to furnish proof of his wrong-doing in a single instance, their accusations will have to be heavily discounted, if not entirely set aside.

In spite of Lorenzo beginning his rule in the same unofficial capacity as his father and grandfather before him, he succeeded in fortifying his position far beyond anything to which they had ever aspired. The occasion for the alteration he effected, which was in its sum a broad constitutional revision in a monarchical sense, was supplied by the unfortunate war which developed (1478-1480) on the heels of the Pazzi Conspiracy. The disasters suffered in this conflict, waged largely on Tuscan soil, released sharp criticism in the councils, which were still, as they had ever been, the outstanding popular feature of the constitution. The demonstration against his regime greatly alarmed Lorenzo, and no sooner had he escaped destruction at the hands of Pope Sixtus IV and King Ferrante by his bold visit to Naples than he resolved to effect constitutional changes calculated to sap the vigor of the popular features still imbedded in the system.

He had hardly made his triumphal return from Naples when, on April 8, 1480, he attacked the problem by the measure which in Florence regularly initiated a "reform." He summoned a controlled parliament which granted sweeping powers to a committee of its or rather of Lorenzo's private nomination. The committee, or balìa, after the usual elaborate legerdemain, drew the usual rabbit from its magical hat. This surprise animal was a new council, the Council of Seventy, authorized to supersede all existing councils, without however definitely and finally replacing them. In constitutionally conservative Florence nothing once established was ever abolished, even though it no longer functioned in any effective sense.

The Council of Seventy was meant to become, and became, the heart of the government. Its members sat for life, they filled vacancies in their ranks by co-optation, and all power in the state was concentrated in their hands. While a consensus of opinion was assured by the solidly Medicean character of the membership, still seventy individuals constitute too many-headed a government to act with efficiency and dispatch. Consequently, the Seventy delegated their most essential powers to two permanent committees. One of these, the Eight, was intrusted with foreign affairs and military matters, the other, the Twelve, dealt with financial and commercial interests. It is permissible to think of the Seventy as a self-perpetuating senate served by two working committees appointed from its membership. The old councils, which, as already said, were not abolished, retained the privilege of approving the measures voted by the Seventy. Nor was the signory composed of gonfalonier and priors abolished. Appointed by the Seventy for the unchanged bimestrial period, it continued to sit in the palace as the ornamental figurehead of the still nominally republican ship of state.

The most striking feature of the whole constitutional hocus-pocus was the improvement it effected of Lorenzo's control. The Medicean rule, so long carefully concealed, was at last publically unveiled; for Lorenzo himself sat among the Seventy and was directly or indirectly represented on the two committees charged with the most important executive functions. There can be no doubt that with these changes something resembling a monarchy had begun to emerge. But the fact that the old forms, as hollowed out as a forest of dead oaks, were left standing testifies to a public state of mind which obliged Lorenzo not entirely to abandon the traditional Medicean anonymity and to refrain from too visibly playing the signore.

Lorenzo had hardly reached his manhood years when he began to feel the first twinges of the disease which for generations had been the plague of his family. The physicians, defining it as gout, recommended for its cure a season at one of the many warm baths that dotted the neighborhood. As these gave him at best but temporary relief, he steadily declined from year to year so that long before he was forty he was frequently obliged to withdraw from public view for an extended period. It is a striking fact that his affliction hardly, if at all, impaired the exuberant energy which was his natural heritage. He loved life in the country and was much of his time on the move among the villas inherited from his father. It was Poggio a Cajano, however, a magnificent estate of his own creation in the rolling pastoral country toward Pistoia, which he favored above all others. Enamored of horses and dogs, he took inexhaustible delight in hunting and hawking and in one of his liveliest poems has left us a radiant account of a day spent at the latter of these sports. His unbounded vitality expressed itself also in well-documented sexual excesses and led to numerous infidelities, which his devoted wife schooled herself to ignore. Daughter of a Roman condottiere of high degree, she was not a woman of great intelligence but was kindly and conventionally religious and presided with dignity over her large family. She bore her husband many children, of whom three boys and three girls survived her own early death at the age of thirty-eight, four years before that of her overpowering mate.

To Lorenzo, head of what had virtually become an Italian dynasty, the marriage of his children became a matter of the greatest importance. Not only was it desirable to match them to partners of their own or of superior station, but each union was expected to add some element of strength to the mounting house of Medici. Accordingly, his daughters Lucrezia and Contessina were married respectively to a Salviati and a Ridolfi, both members of leading families of Florence. For the third daughter, Maddalena, he chose the son of Pope Innocent VIII, successor of the rancorous Sixtus IV. This was a peculiarly shrewd move in matrimonial diplomacy, since it allied him with the papacy, for which, following his disastrous clash with Sixtus, he had developed an unlimited respect. Moreover, he was not handing over his daughter to a papal bastard, which would have been a blow to his pride, since Francesco Cibò was the legitimate son of his father by a marriage he had contracted before he had taken clerical orders.

The marriage of his oldest son and prospective heir, Piero, called for an even more careful scrutiny of the available market wares. Perhaps under wife Clarice's influence the choice fell on a girl of her own Orsini family, Alfonsina by name. Exactly as in the case of his sisters, Piero's marriage took place at what, according to present-day standards, would be called an extremely early age. He was only seventeen years old when Alfonsina left Rome to live with him as his wife in the Medici palace.

There remain to be considered two sons, Giovanni and Giuliano, of whom Giuliano was still too young to have any plan formed in his behalf. Giovanni's case, however, assumed such importance for the later fortunes of the house that it needs to be closely scanned. The circumspect statesman Lorenzo came to the conviction that no conceivable event could give his family such a lift as would its representation in the college of cardinals. He could not but have been struck with the fact that as soon as in the past any family of the peninsula had surged to the front politically, it had managed to place one of its members in that exalted company. Not only did the appointee then sit as in a tower commanding an incomparable survey of the contemporary world of strife and intrigue, but there was always the chance that he might emerge from a conclave following the demise of a pope as the dead incumbent's successor.

Immediately on the election to the papacy of Innocent VIII in 1484, Lorenzo took the first step toward the realization of his ambition by cultivating the most cordial relations with him. A giant forward stride was effected when, four years later, he persuaded the pope to bless the nuptials of his son, Francesco Cibò, and Lorenzo's daughter, Maddalena. Therewith the Magnificent had achieved a family intimacy which made it easy for him to press the case of his son Giovanni on the pope's attention. Giovanni had from his earliest youth been destined by his father for a clerical career and to the father's joy had proved himself an unusually studious and well behaved young man. So persistently did Lorenzo ply the pope with the request that Giovanni be made a cardinal that Innocent at last gave way. This was in 1489, when Giovanni was only fourteen years old. Beset, however, by scruples, which even a Renaissance pope could not entirely escape, the papal benefactor added a reservation to the effect that Giovanni was not to exercise the authority conferred by his office for three more years.

Accordingly, in March, 1492, amidst festivities of exceptional splendor all Florence joined in acclaiming the newest prince of the church. It does not appear that his youth gave any offense to that callous age, although, viewed in the light of the more honorable tradition of the church, it constituted a scandal of the first order. That the bed-rid Lorenzo was unable to take part in the public rejoicings cast a shadow over them, of which only a few of his oldest and closest friends took note. Like the gallant gentleman he was he bade a cheerful fare-

well to his son on Giovanni's setting out for Rome to take the
exalted seat to which he had been appointed and then contrived
to summon the strength to dispatch to him a long last letter of
instruction.[1] It was not very different in substance from the
kind of advice anxious fathers through the ages have given their
sons to the end of guiding their footsteps over the difficult social
terrain they were essaying for the first time. Lord Chesterfield's
counsels to his son have a strong family likeness to those of
Lorenzo and, to adduce a supreme literary example, so do those
of Polonius to Laertes. The most interesting light the letter throws
on Lorenzo is the disclosure of his uncompromising realism.
He paints the contemporary Roman society as the cesspool that
every Italian knew it to be and hopes and prays that his son
may by enlightened foreknowledge escape from falling into it.

Shortly after Giovanni's departure from Florence, Lorenzo,
knowing that his end was not far off, had himself carried to
his nearby country seat at Careggi. He wished to die where his
father and grandfather had died before him. So rapidly, as the
ecstatic Tuscan spring once more came up from the south, did
his strength wane that on an early April day a priest was summoned to administer the last rites. Lorenzo's closest friend, the
humanist and poet, Angelo Poliziano, was in constant attend-
ance, the young and handsome scholar, Pico della Mirandola,
paid him a moving visit of farewell. In a long session with his
son, Piero, he discussed the many political problems of the city,
while concealing as best he could the disturbing doubts which
he, like all who knew Piero, entertained of that arrogant young
man. Suddenly there was ushered into the bedchamber the
famous Dominican friar, Girolamo Savonarola, prior of San
Marco monastery. In the after years his visit became the subject
of so acrimonious a controversy that we cannot pass it by, even
though for its proper grasp we are obliged to go back to the
friar's first appearance on the Florentine scene.

✦

[1] A translation is to be found in Roscoe, *Lorenzo de' Medici*, II, 427-430 (ed. of 1825).

Girolamo Savonarola was a native of Ferrara who under an irresistible spiritual compulsion became a Dominican friar. After due training at a monastery of his order at Bologna, he was sent as a preacher on a round of missions through Tuscany. His first appearance at Florence was a flat failure. However, on returning to the city in 1490, he scored an unexampled success by sermons, first at the monastery of St. Mark's and, later, in the more capacious cathedral, wherein he passionately denounced the corruption of the church and with equal fervor predicted its approaching purification. Not since the Middle Ages had such unrestrained damnation of the wicked ways of the world been heard from a Christian pulpit. Elected prior of San Marco by the thrilled brothers, he presented immediate further evidence of his uncompromising temper by refusing to pay the customary visit of respect to Lorenzo de' Medici as the hereditary patron of the monastery. It was this demonstrative hostility which makes his appearance at the ruler's deathbed something of a mystery. The most plausible explanation is that Lorenzo, who had been deeply impressed with the prior's unbending rectitude, had expressed a desire for his presence. A few weeks later, Poliziano, eye-witness of the interview, spoke of it in a letter to a friend in which he recounted at some length the story of Lorenzo's last days. Arrived at Savonarola's visit, he says that the prior summoned the dying man to repentance and, on departing, at Lorenzo's instance, gave him his blessing.

This, as the only version of the event by an eye-witness, would have become the unchallenged historical account, had not a far more colorful story gained currency some years later after Savonarola's life had run its course and he had suffered death by fire in the great public square of Florence. Thousands of men and women, chiefly of the poor and burdened classes, had never wavered in their faith in him as a prophet sent by God and fervently nursed their dream after he was gone. Precisely as in comparable cases of blind devotion throughout history the followers of Savonarola fell victim to delusions and freely revised the past of their worshiped leader in the burning light of their reading of his mission. Out of this feverish state of mind there gradually emerged a version of the surprising deathbed visit of their sainted guide for which there is no authority beyond a rumor circulating among the grieved and abandoned friars of San Marco after their master's tragic exit from the world.

While it is difficult to the point of impossibility to accept this prejudiced Dominican version as the true story of the puzzling deathbed scene, it was so generally accepted at the time and has ever since made so persistent an appearance in the histories dealing with the event that it cannot be denied a place in a record of Lorenzo's life. So here it is, though in considerably abbreviated form. Before Savonarola, arrived at Lorenzo's bedside, would consent to shrive him, he demanded that the penitent satisfy three demands. The first was that he should affirm his adherence to the true faith. This Lorenzo did and was next required to promise to restore all unjustly appropriated property. (This is generally held to have reference to the supposedly plundered public funds.) To this, too, the dying man consented and was then confronted with the third and supreme demand that he restore the stolen liberty of Florence. On Lorenzo's indicating his refusal by turning his face to the wall, the man of God consigned the sinner to eternal fire by abruptly taking his departure.

However belated in making its appearance, this was a version of the departure from the mundane scene of a famous but debatable political figure to the accompaniment of religious thunder to which the heart of man has never failed to respond. No cause for wonder therefore that the Savonarolist version has all but crowded the better verified earlier report from the pages of history.

Lorenzo died in the early night hours of Sunday, April 8, 1492. With simple ceremonies that scrupulously avoided all unnecessary display, he was buried in the ancestral church of

San Lorenzo. If life is reckoned by richness of experience rather than by length of days, he must, in spite of his death at the early age of forty-three, be considered to have had an enviable existence. As to the admiration and affection of the mass of the Florentines there can be no doubt, although a small, stubborn opposition never ceased to gnaw at his reputation. Only rarely, however, has the favorable opinion of the contemporary generation been dissipated so speedily. When two years after his demise his unfortunate son and heir, Piero, was driven out of Florence, the succeeding republican rulers promptly consigned Lorenzo to oblivion, and never afterward has his reputation experienced a sufficiently confident revival for his countrymen to have felt moved to perpetuate his memory by a monument adequately expressive of his worth.

X

LORENZO AS HUMANIST, POET, PATRON, AND RULER

IN LORENZO'S time the humanist movement reached a peak, due largely to Lorenzo himself. While continuing the by now traditional family role of patron, he added to the volume and vigor of the humanist stream by direct, creative participation. We have noted that from its origin humanism expressed itself in the two distinct yet related fields of scholarship and literature. Turning to scholarship first, let us briefly recall that it set itself the task of discovering lost and multiplying existent manuscripts, of establishing the original text of the classical works which the carelessness of a long succession of scribes had impaired, and of giving as wide a currency as possible to the secular viewpoint native to the recovered literature.

As long as the spread of humanism depended on the slow and expensive process of producing books by hand, its pace was necessarily hampered. Then an event occurred which vastly accelerated its diffusion. A little past the middle of the fifteenth century, in the Rhine country, there befell the revolutionary invention of printing with movable type. As soon as the new art had been transplanted to Italy, which happened with little delay, changes of incalculable significance followed. The first book printed at Florence appeared in 1471, at the very beginning of Lorenzo's rule. Almost over night presses were set up in all the towns of Italy and a wave of humanist popularization washed over the country. Two outstanding consequences were that the demand for books increased by leaps and bounds and that it was no longer only the rich and powerful who might aspire to acquire a library.

However, at least as important as the expansion of the book market was the capture of the often buried meaning of the books through organized study. This would be a service appertaining to the university, and Lorenzo, conscious of his obligation as the promoter of higher education, promptly enlarged the facilities with which the university of Florence had been hitherto content. In his day there taught at the local institution the most learned and stimulating body of humanists to be found anywhere in the peninsula. Cristoforo Landino held the chair of rhetoric and poetry, Marsilio Ficino discoursed on philosophy, Demetrius Chalcondylas taught Greek, and Poliziano, by general consent the leading classical scholar of the age, served as professor of Latin and Greek eloquence.

An act of Lorenzo, coming under the head of what we may call educational statesmanship, needs to be mentioned at this point. With the republic of Florence aspiring to become territorially identical with Tuscany, Lorenzo could only at his peril neglect the interests of the towns that had come under its rule. Of these quite the most important was Pisa, which since its conquest in 1406 had sunk into a visible and distressful decay. Not content with efforts to promote its commercial revival, Lorenzo took the further step of endowing it with a university, even though its establishment would inescapably diminish the importance of the university of Florence and thereby arouse the resentment of his fellow townsmen. For what he had to do, in view of the fact that his state was too small to support two full-grown universities, was to distribute the faculties appertaining to a single institution between the two towns in such a way that, while Florence retained the newer humanist studies, the more traditional departments of law, medicine, and theology were transferred to Pisa. So capably were the Pisan faculties staffed under Lorenzo's direct supervision that they promptly drew a considerable student body to the moribund town and thus served the double purpose of augmenting the reputation of his state as a center of learning and of helping to reanimate the languishing coastal city.

In the eyes of contemporaries and, even more decidedly in the eyes of later generations down to the threshold of the twentieth century, Florence harbored an institution in Lorenzo's time which, as humanist in purpose as the university, exercised a much wider and subtler empire throughout Italy. This was the Platonic Academy which, as we know, owed its material origin to Cosimo and its spiritual significance to its acknowledged high priest, Marsilio Ficino. But while conceding to the Academy an influence which supplemented and enforced that of the university, it is only by a complete misapprehension as to its manner of functioning that it is thought of in terms of an institution at all. Far from having a definite organization and engaging in the various activities we are in the habit of associating with a learned academy, it expressed itself collectively through nothing more impressive than an occasional, informal gathering of men with a common interest in the philosopher, Plato, and with a common faith in the guidance of Marsilio Ficino, who had dedicated his life to the ancient Athenian. A further bond among the members of the circle was their attachment to Lorenzo de' Medici, without whom they might not even have had their rare sessions, since it was he who usually brought them about by inviting his philosophizing associates to a banquet at his villa at Careggi. Having in his youth enjoyed the instruction of Ficino, the Magnificent had come to share the tutor's regard for his worshiped idol. Nor did this indicate an intellectual

drift at all uncommon in that period. For the dominant humanist thinkers throughout Italy looked on the older scholastics,
whom they had superseded, as their inveterate foes and were
pleased to speed the passing of scholasticism by exalting the
mystical Plato over the rational Aristotle, whom scholasticism
revered as the beginning and end of wisdom.

To what, then, since the Academy functioned chiefly as an
occasional banquet of congenial spirits is the very considerable
influence it exercised to be attributed? The answer is simple.
The message of the Academy reached the growing body of readers through the publications of its leading members. Head and
front of these was of course Ficino. His most decisive contribution was his Latin version of the Athenian's works, the publica-
tion of which he had begun just before the death of Cosimo,
his earliest benefactor. By 1477 the vast enterprise was completed, and a few years later Plato's *opera omnia* could be purchased in a magnificent edition produced by the new art of
multiple book-making.

Ficino supplemented his editorial work with critical essays
and was seconded in these propaganda labors by his university
colleague, Landino, whose conversion to Platonism under his
friend Ficino's influence was without reservation. But a late-
comer and non-Florentine also figured in the labors of diffusion.
This was Pico della Mirandola, who, on settling in Florence toward the middle of Lorenzo's rule, was universally regarded,
although only just emerging from adolescence, as the epitome
of all learning. It is easy at the present day to see that the reputation which Pico enjoyed during his short lifetime and which,
if anything, grew after his death, was artificially inflated by
claims which have been sadly punctured by later investigations.
He boasted, for instance, or his friends boasted for him, that
he had mastered twenty-two languages. It has turned out on
closer scrutiny that his knowledge of these tongues in most
cases covered little more than familiarity with their alphabets.
Admittedly, however, his hunger for learning knew no bounds

and to the unrestrained admiration of his contemporaries embraced the wisdom of the Arabs, the Cabbala of the Jews, and every form of ancient and medieval philosophy, including of course the Platonism of Ficino, to whom, like Landino and Lorenzo himself, he was ardently attached.

Every present-day university graduate who has occupied himself at all seriously with the movement of philosophy through the ages will quickly discover that what Ficino, Landino, and Pico della Mirandola dished out in their time as Platonism was a completely unscholarly hodge-podge. Its central and fundamental defect was that what it offered as Platonism was not the doctrine of the Athenian sage of the fourth century B.C. but a capriciously distorted version thereof developed four hundred years later at Alexandria in Egypt and commonly called Neoplatonism. This later and perverted form of Platonism was already so abundantly superstitious and darkly mystical that it falls completely apart under systematic rational attack. Uncritically taken over by the Florentine Platonists of the quattrocento, it became a hopeless farrago, wherein stray passages from the Alexandrians were mingled with the loose imaginings of their own excited and undisciplined minds. The commonly entertained idea which set these men off on their daring sky-flights was that all the religions and philosophies of the past professed an identical God and that this God was indistinguishable from the God of Christianity. This conviction, astir in them as a blind, activating faith, enabled them to deduce from the oneness of God the oneness of mankind. Heartening as this teaching was in itself, it was invalidated by reason of the monstrous distortion of the evidence practiced in order to establish it.

If we contented ourselves with this scathing judgment on Florentine Platonism, its gaining so great a following and ruling so many noble minds would remain forever unintelligible. Let it therefore be promptly confessed that although the method employed to identify the God of all peoples and ages as the same, as indeed the Christian, deity was faulty, a universal creator did issue from the argument together with the conviction that the force that impelled him to his uninterrupted creativity was love. Love therefore rules the universe, laying the obligation on the individual soul imbedded in matter, which is Evil, to find its way back to its divine source, the only conceivable and undebatable Good. Unhappily there is a false, an animal love, which inheres in the senses and the flesh. This, destined to plague us during our mortal span, it is our duty to subdue and conquer. To every individual soul during its mortal pilgrimage there comes the call to choose between the animal and the spiritual love and, as it chooses, it is lost or saved.

It will at once appear that the love doctrine of the Florentine Platonists hardly differs by a shade from the love doctrine of mystical Christianity and that this identity is the real reason for the great vogue which it achieved. For at the side of the elegant semi-paganism which figured so prominently in the intellectual foreground of the age, there continued to persist among many of the finest spirits the old medieval search of God, to which the Platonic teachings with their new and different approach gave fresh stimulation. The mystic love doctrine, compounded of Platonism and Christianity, may therefore be encountered in much of the most characteristic and prized expression of the day. An outstanding example is furnished by the sonnets of Michelangelo, of which it is the sustaining fire. Again, it so deeply penetrated Baldassare Castiglione that, when he projected the ideal gentleman in his famous *Il Cortigiano,* he assigned the final shaping influence to Platonic love. It dominated also the most tender and tortured spirit of the age, the painter Botticelli. Much of his intensely introspective musing turned about the current teaching and induced him to inspired utterance in two of the most admired allegories of modern art. They are the "Birth of Venus" (Venus being love's impersonator) and the "Realm of Venus," which passes under the popular misnomer of "Spring." The flowered girlish figure of "Spring" in this latter allegory has understandably captured the imagination of the succeeding generations. But she is not the theme song of the picture. She is merely the fairest inhabitant of the kingdom of Venus who, in her role of queen, is presented as unmistakably ruling the world which the canvas projects.

With humanism sternly imposing the use of the Latin language as the only appropriate medium for literary expression, the native Italian movement so vigorously inaugurated by Dante, Petrarch, and Boccaccio went into a decline from which it did not recover until the period of Lorenzo. And the note that cannot be too strongly sounded is that it was Lorenzo's personal initiative which more than any other single factor awakened Italian literature from its long torpor. When on his father Piero's death, he assumed the political control which he at once combined with cultural leadership, the Latin obsession still ruled the best minds and made Latin the obligatory medium not only for scholars in their learned communications addressed to other scholars but also for literary aspirants and, especially, poets, who sought the wider public congenial to their message.

Angelo Poliziano will serve as an instance to show how the Latin obsession worked. We have encountered him so far in two capacities: he was Lorenzo's friend and housemate and he stood out as a leading figure in the group of scholars constituting the glory of the humanist faculty at Florence. By general agreement he was the foremost classical philologist of his day who, in respect of precision and breadth of scholarship, outstripped all his rivals. However, not only in his communications stemming from his learned activities did he, as might be expected, employ the Latin tongue but also in the poetry to which, being a man of parts, he presently turned for relaxation. He tried his hand at odes, elegies, and other classical verse-forms and in all of them achieved an external perfection which won him unstinted praise. It was said of him, and can be easily believed, that he carried his mastery of both Latin and Greek so far that he not only imitatively wrote and talked but actually and creatively thought in these acquired tongues.

The humanists from the first had aspired to nothing higher than to be the imitators and apes of the incomparable ancients. No one so fully realized this unfortunate aim as Poliziano with consequences that might well serve as a warning for all time to writers similarly prompted. For, in measure as he perfected himself in classical syntax, diction, and metaphor he became progressively empty of personal content and in the long run disclosed himself to the disenchanted ear as no better than a tinkling cymbal. Under Lorenzo's influence he was in his later life persuaded to follow his friend's example and to resort for poetic expression also to the lowly Italian vehicle. The vernacular verse, to which he then gave utterance, has the precise merits and defects of his Latin efforts, which may be succinctly summarized as external perfection coupled with internal hollowness.

So long as the Latin enslavement lasted, and it was not totally cast off for another century, Poliziano was celebrated by the historians of humanism as the leading poet of the Laurentian Age. Only slowly did originality achieve a higher rating among readers than successful imitation, and only after this fresher insight had become general was the literary primacy once accorded to Poliziano transferred to Lorenzo. It was characteristic of the Tuscan rootedness of this son of Florence and indicative of his spontaneous preference for the living waters of poetry that, in spite of his classical education, he never hesitated, when it came to giving utterance to the feelings with which he overflowed, to resort to the immediate medium of his mother tongue. In an essaylike letter written when he was only seventeen years old to his friend, Federigo of Naples, he set forth in glowing terms the merits of the poetry of Dante and Petrarch. It had, he confessed, been regretfully pushed into the background, but he hoped to have its honor restored by a second birth in his time. He enclosed four poems of his own in sonnet form as evidence of high resolve and continued thereafter as long as he lived to utilize the sonnet as the form best suited to disclose some passing mood or special situation related to the sentiment of love.

Lorenzo's love poetry tailored to the inherited sonnet form is abundant but neither very original nor very important. One reason for its failure to come alive may well have been that the sonnet was a literary device of which Petrarch had already exhausted the possibilities; another even more convincing reason would seem to be that the sonnet of Lorenzo's time still fed on a medieval concept which by the fifteenth century had been worn to a shadow. According to this concept, which originated with the poetry of chivalry, the proper inspiration of all true love poetry was an ideal lady, a mere dream figure, at home somewhere in the unfathomed sky and glimpsed only in moments of high exaltation or through a veil of tears. Not until Lorenzo turned to nature as his theme did he find himself the possessor of an indubitable poetic voice. Endowed with lively senses and sharply responsive to every change of weather and the seasons, he was never more completely himself than when residing at one of his country estates engaged in looking over his herds, improving his stud, racing the fields for the pure exhilaration of the exercise, or carrying out some hawking or hunting expedition with a company of friends.

The three poems commonly accounted as his best are: *Ambra, Caccia col Falcone,* and *Nencia da Barberino,* and even the briefest statement of their content will disclose that they sprang easily and spontaneously from his quickening contact with the Tuscan countryside. *Ambra* employs a somewhat shop-worn Ovidian framework to celebrate the natural beauties of Poggio a Cajano, the villa of his own creation in which he delighted above all others. The *Caccia col Falcone* is a brilliantly impressionistic description of a day spent at hawking; and the *Nencia da Barberino* is a homely and locally flavored version of the classical eclogue. Its central figure is a peasant who sings the charms of his peasant mistress with a fine sincerity which is heightened rather than impaired by humorous bucolic touches and comparisons.

Lorenzo also distinguished himself in a form of poetry of a distinctly Florentine and urban character. From the earliest period of Christianity, the Italian towns, with Florence making no exception, had, in the season preceding Lent, made ready to bid the flesh farewell with vivacious and often exceedingly gross explosions of song and general merrymaking. By the time of Lorenzo the pre-Lenten extravagances had degenerated into such disorderly outbursts of vulgar obscenity that the disgusted Lorenzo resolved to raise them to a higher level by recasting them in the form of allegorical pageants with appropriate declamations, costumes, and music. He composed some of the literature for these occasions himself and understandably retained, for he was an esthetic and distinctly not a moral reformer, much of the unrestrained expression that furnished the traditional flavor of the seasonal event. Puritanical critics have not failed to level their shafts at the *ballate* and carnival songs that carry his hallmark. In rebuttal it is pertinent to point out that critics of that stripe usually have a defective sense of historical change and that for them to demand of Lorenzo that he should not behave as a traditional Florentine is a moral and mental absurdity. His perhaps leading trait was an immediacy which conceded to each passing moment its particular glow and which extracted a special poignancy from the knowledge that the glow was tragically ephemeral. The consciousness that joy is momentary and inescapably attended by its yoke-fellow, sorrow, is admirably conveyed by the most frequently cited quatrain of his carnival verse:

> *Quant'è bella giovinezza,*
> *Che si fugge tuttavia!*
> *Chi vuol esser lieto, sia:*
> *Di doman non c'è certezza.*[1]

[1] *Fair is youth and free of sorrow,*
Yet how soon its joys we bury.
Let who would be now be merry:
Sure is no one of tomorrow.

No one may doubt that Lorenzo gladly assumed the patronage of letters and art traditional in his family, although the details of his patronage do not always present themselves clearly to view. It is easier to follow his support of letters than of art, for he was, as already related, not only closely associated with both the scholars and writers of his day but ended by rising to leadership among them as their most creative figure.

As to the wide range of his cultural interests there can be no doubt, for he extended his favor to every form of art and every variety of craft. The Medici palace became in his time a standing exhibit of contemporary furniture, majolicas, and bronzes, and its collection of gems, cameos, and medals, ancient and modern, was celebrated throughout Italy. The numerous guests of the house would immediately on their arrival inquire about it, or, in case they failed to do so, would be sure to have their host press it on their attention. Lorenzo set particular store by his museum of casts and fragments of actual ancient sculpture, which to make accessible to the public and, particularly, to the young followers of the arts, he assembled in a garden along the via Larga not far from the palace. It was there one day that he encountered young Michelangelo and found himself so greatly impressed with the lad's appearance and talent that he invited him to live as guest under his roof and share a place at his table. Without this princely hospitality, Michelangelo, whose father could barely feed his large family, would not have been able to pursue his studies. An interesting aftermath of this generous intervention in his behalf was that when, in his later years, like the Florentines in general, Michelangelo renounced the Medici as tyrants, he could never quite bring himself to sponge out the debt he owed his magnanimous earliest patron.

It is likely that, owing to his straitened financial circumstances, Lorenzo did not scatter commissions among the architects, sculptors, and painters of his generation on the same lavish scale as his grandfather. Still, he moved in their company

with pleasure and set its individual members to work according
to his available resources. It is a tribute to his fine artistic discrimination that among the sculptors he favored Verrocchio,
among the painters, Botticelli, each in Lorenzo's day the outstanding figure in his chosen field. A more distinctly Florentine
artist than Verrocchio it is difficult to conceive, and to consider
no more than the labors he performed at Lorenzo's orders is to
come face to face with the art of the quattrocento at its peak.
Among them is the imposing porphyry sarcophagus with its
delicate wrought-iron tracery in the sacristy of San Lorenzo
which holds the mortal remains of the Magnificent's father and
uncle. Then, in the Museo Nazionale, will be found the bronze
figure of the young David with drawn sword who, having just
severed Goliath's head from his body, is seized with sudden shy-
ness over a deed beyond his age and power. And finally, forever
unforgettable for every visitor of the Palazzo Vecchio, there in
the entrance court is the bronze fountain figure of the laughing
boy struggling not to let the slithery, spouting dolphin slip from
his insecure grasp.

Verrocchio's most famous work was also his last: the equestrian
statue of the condottiere, Colleoni. It was done at the order,
not of Lorenzo or even of Florence, but at the command of
the proud rival city of Venice. The high-riding, insolent bronze
horseman owes the vast reputation he has enjoyed through all
the subsequent centuries down to our day to his having imposed
himself on the imagination as the perfect expression of the
Italian Renaissance. That constitutes his deserved immortality.
However, for the lover of the natively flavored genius of Verrocchio, the earlier works done at Lorenzo's instigation have a more
intimately revealing quality.

That Sandro Botticelli lived closely not only with Lorenzo
but with the whole Neoplatonic circle has already been noted
in connection with his two famous pictorial representations of
Venus, goddess of Love. Another of his allegories, more especially
of interest to the historian, celebrates the Magnificent's suc-

cessful emergence from the terrible Pazzi crisis. Its subject is Pallas Athena (Wisdom) taming the Centaur (Barbarism and War). It was composed to commemorate the hazardous journey Lorenzo made to Naples to terminate a conflict which was engulfing him and his state in inescapable ruin. Specific reference to the occasion which gave birth to the canvas will be found in the multiple linked rings which adorn the costume of the goddess and which are Lorenzo's personal device. Another revealing detail is the glimpse of the gulf of Naples which constitutes the background of the picture.

It cannot be justly said that the Pallas Athena allegory ranks among Botticelli's best works nor that, born a free and far-ranging spirit, the master ever fell into anything approaching servile dependence on his patron. For the biographer of Lorenzo it suffices to record that he honored himself by living in intimate relationship with the most subtle artist of his time. To come, however, to an adequate understanding of Botticelli it would be necessary to study him in the whole long catalogue of his works and lovingly to indicate the successive phases by which he manifested his incomparable genius. And for such an exposition this chapter, concerned solely with Lorenzo in his capacity of patron, is manifestly not the place.

Any final estimate of Lorenzo must begin by signalizing him as the most notable link in the Medici succession, the finest flowering to which the family attained. If he played his part on too circumscribed a stage to allot him a place in the small group of men who figure as the makers and shakers of history, he commanded a sum of talents and covered a range of activities that at least convincingly establish his claim to be numbered among the outstanding men of his age. We have followed his career as Florentine ruler and Italian statesman and have noted that, far from contenting himself with his absorbing political tasks, he was a passionate sportsman, personally looked after his many farm properties, actively cultivated the classical and philosophical movements of his generation, patronized the arts and crafts with a rare discrimination, and, after spurring Italian literature to new efforts, led the way by his own works to a fresh outburst of native poetry. This by the standard of any period constitutes a record that has not often been excelled.

His continuous immersion in so tumultuous a stream of interests bears witness to what reveals itself as his leading trait, an unquenchable zest for life. Instead of his many activities getting into each other's way, each stimulated its neighbor for the simple reason that they all issued from a vigorous and harmonious personality. Consequently, he had the capacity to give himself easily and without confusion to the many separate interests that made up his average day. It was not at all unusual for him in the course of a single morning to write or dictate a dozen letters, to draw up instructions for an ambassador departing on an important mission, to join a discussion among experts of a moot doctrine of Greek philosophy, to examine a medal or cameo with a view to adding it to his collection, and to make the arrangements for a happy hunting expedition with a group of friends. Like the Italians generally, he was not inhibited by an awkward self-consciousness but was of an open nature, courteous, and accessible to high and low alike. Thus readily and graciously identified with the most characteristic thought and actions of his countrymen, he deserves more by reason of his radiant personality than by his authority as ruler and statesman to have his period called the Laurentian Age.

Although following the revamping of the constitution in 1480 he was more effectively the sole ruler, the tyrant, of the Florentine commonwealth than his father and grandfather had been, he must never be confounded with the stark and violent usurpers of power to be encountered in his time throughout the rest of the peninsula. It clearly marks the chasm between them and him that he interpreted the humanism to which he was devoted not only as a new and stimulating form of intellectuality but also as a nobler social order, under which the surviving remnants of feudal barbarism would be replaced by a code of softer and more urbane relationships. He was therefore, although exercising a form of tyranny, a ruler eminently humane and free from rancor. Among his earliest acts was the recall from exile of the families that had been the victims of the revolution that had put his grandfather, Cosimo, at the head of the government. Among the beneficiaries of this clemency were the Albizzi, descendants of the heads of the oligarchic party which the Medici had displaced. Time and chance had reduced them to an insignificant remnant and they never again surged to the front. The return of the Strozzi, who had been involved in the downfall of the Albizzi, took a different turn. One of its exiled members had started a bank at Naples and had amassed a fortune. On his return he wisely refrained from prosecuting the ancient feud with the result that he and his descendants after him took a conspicuous part in the later history of the city.

Even more revealing of Lorenzo's fine civic temper was his treatment of the Pazzi. When, on the failure of the conspiracy for which native opinion held them chiefly responsible, the infuriated mob yielded to the impulse of indiscriminate murder, he exerted all his influence to set a term to its madness. Its rage against the traitorous family knew no bounds and called for nothing less than its total extermination. Except for old Jacopo, the head of the house, and his nephew, Francesco, who were savagely butchered, the others were rescued from the itching hands of the rioters by Lorenzo putting them under protective arrest and interning them in the distant fortress of Volterra. A younger brother of the murdered Francesco, Guglielmo by name, was married to Bianca, one of Lorenzo's sisters. Left uninformed of the conspiracy by his guilty brother and uncle, Guglielmo was of course innocent and, taken under his brother-in-law's wing, was not even put under restraint. It is plain that Lorenzo refused to consider himself involved in an old-fashioned blood-feud with the Pazzi, who were one of the most ancient and honorable families of the town. Instead of indulging the urge of vengeance which must have been the first response to the murder of his brother, he looked forward to and actually planned an eventual reconciliation, which he then inaugurated, two years after the incarceration at Volterra, by ordering the release of the prisoners.

As crowning confirmation of Lorenzo's humane rule we have the many references to it by visiting Italians of other allegiances. They are of one mind in declaring that Florence enjoyed a better civil order and a greater security of life and goods than any other community of the peninsula. Let the single testimony of an otherwise unimportant contemporary stand for that of all the rest. Said he: "In no other part of Italy do people observe a higher standard of conduct. There are here no robberies, no nocturnal commotions, no assassinations." [1]

The striking mental and moral balance which defines Lorenzo's unique personality enabled him successfully to blend the Catholicism into which he was born with the humanism which was the substance of his education. He never fell into the extremes of a radical wing of his contemporaries who let themselves be persuaded that to adopt the free outlook of the ancients necessitated the rejection of the Christian faith. Never at any time did he join in the sophisticated gibing on the part of many members of his circle of intimates at orthodox believers who continued to lean on the spiritual support afforded by mass and confessional. His earnest and unfaltering concern was to bring about that fusion of ancient thought and medieval faith which was the best hope of a healthily expanding European culture.

Memorable as were the achievements of this richly endowed personality, there was one thing it did not achieve, for, fortunate as Lorenzo was in the main, he failed to attain what toward the close of his rule had become his supreme political objective. This was to create an Italian sentiment among the states of the peninsula strong enough to induce them to give up their

[1] Roscoe, *Lorenzo de' Medici*, II, 43-44.

petty animosities in order to present a united front to the threatening invasion of the king of France. As if driven by a blind will to suicide, the rulers of these states took turns in playing with the thought of the king's descent among them in the expectation of getting from him as helper of his expedition some inconsequential advantage over local rivals. Lorenzo lived just long enough to witness the decisive last move in this game of monumental folly. In the month of February preceding his death in April, 1492, Lodovico Sforza, who had stolen the duchy of Milan from his young nephew, the rightful duke, sent a richly appointed embassy to the French court to solicit an early intervention in Italian affairs. It communicated the final impetus to King Charles VIII's wavering intentions. He ordered the acceleration of the military preparations that had for some time been under way and in the year 1494 led a French army across the Alps which in numbers and equipment completely dwarfed everything in this kind the puny Italian states had hitherto witnessed. The invasion marked the beginning of the enslavement of Italy; it also initiated the coming of the slow fog which dimmed and, finally, blotted out the brilliant culture of the peninsula.

THE OVERTHROW OF PIERO II FOLLOWED BY
THE REPUBLICAN INTERLUDE OF 1494-1512

ON LORENZO'S death his oldest son, Piero, named for his grandfather and therefore conveniently designated Piero II, took over his father's unofficial rule without any protest from any quarter. The brevity of his reign, reckoned in months rather than years, has often been attributed to his inexperience, for he was but twenty-two years old at his accession, coupled with his uncontrolled temper. This would seem to have stemmed from his Orsini ancestry and raised a barrier between him and his fellow citizens, whom he was mistakenly inclined to regard in the light of subjects. Agreed that his haughtiness and political ineptitude figured in his overthrow, still every discerning analyst of the lowering general situation he faced must unerringly conclude that he could not have saved himself, even had he combined in his single person the talents of all three of his able predecessors. There is no avoiding the conclusion that the Medicean rule was doomed as soon as King Charles VIII of France made good his long pending threat and crossed the Alps into Italy.

Undeniably, however, Piero hastened his downfall by making a wrong decision in connection with the French descent. As we are aware the final impetus to the invasion was supplied by Lodovico Sforza, the usurping duke of Milan, who hoped in this way to be rid of the pressure put on him by the king of Naples in behalf of the true duke, who was the king's son-in-law. As we are also aware, the immediate goal of the French incursion was the kingdom of Naples, to which Charles VIII supposed himself to have a legitimate claim. With the dominant state of northern Italy, Milan, allied with France, the king would have been reasonably sure of a successful push into the peninsula with even an inferior force, but at the head of 60,000 well-disciplined and well-equipped troops his thrust was irresistible. It was on this very score of the strength of the French invader that Piero fell into his capital error. He persuaded himself that the alliance of the three remaining Italian powers, Florence, the pope, and Naples, would prove sufficiently strong to turn back the French advance. He therefore put his trust in this combination and not until King Charles's army had crossed the Apennines into Tuscany without encountering even a semblance of resistance, did he recognize his miscalculation. Gripped by sudden panic, he then precipitately reversed himself.

Toward the end of October, 1494, he hastened to the French camp and, having put himself without reserve into the hands of the king, was obliged to sign a humiliating treaty which required him to hand over all the key fortresses of his dominion to the French. On his return to Florence early in November the outraged people rose against him as of one accord and drove him together with his younger brothers, the nineteen-year-old Cardinal Giovanni, who happened to have been present at Florence at the time, and the fifteen-year-old Giuliano from the city. With the plundering of the Medici palace from cellar to garret the rage of the populace subsided and the way was cleared for the consideration of the form of government best calculated to consolidate the gains of the revolution.

But before this task could be undertaken the relation to the French invaders had to be clarified with a new treaty in replacement of the one signed by the repudiated Piero. On November 17 Charles VIII made a triumphal entry into Florence at the head of his army. A less impressive warrior than the misshapen youth who bestrode a majestic black war-horse could not be imagined. It did not escape the crowds lining the streets that the royal dwarf was clad cap-a-pie in armor and carried his lance at rest—a posture signifying in the military language of the day that in his view he had taken possession of a conquered city. It proved therefore impossible to wring improved terms from him, and before he and his army resumed their southward march, a new treaty had been signed which confirmed the French occupation of all the decisive fortresses of the Florentine state as long as the war should last. The arrangement made Florence a French client and held it in this dependent condition even after the fortresses, as happened only very gradually, had been regained.

While it is not the concern of this book to follow the history of the renewed republic, it will further our understanding of the vicissitudes through which it passed, if we take account of the constitution with which, after the departure of King Charles, the citizens provided themselves following a remarkably short period of debate. Saving a single important modification, it may be characterized as a return to the familiar republic of the past, for it authorized the resumption of the beloved signory of eight priors headed by a gonfalonier of Justice with the perilously short term of office of two months. The provision signified the attainment of the highest offices of state by the largest feasible number of citizens, which, like their ancestors before them, the revolutionary Florentines of 1494 continued to regard as the loftiest goal for a democracy to shoot at. However, passionately set on blocking the return of the Medici, they declared—and this was the outstanding item of constitutional reform—that the ultimate sovereign authority should henceforth reside not in

the parlamentum, which the Medici had employed as a fraudulent device for the perpetuation of their power, but in a new
institution called the Grand Council. Membership in the Grand
Council was accorded to all citizens who boasted among their
ancestors for three generations back as much as a single occupant of one of the major magistracies. This created a body of
three thousand members who, because too numerous to function
effectively, were divided into three groups serving in rotation
each for a period of three months. It defines the high authority
conferred on the Grand Council that it was intrusted with the
legislative power together with the right to elect the successive
bimestrial signories.

Some eight years later, in 1502, the Grand Council resolved
to strengthen the government's executive branch. This was done
by giving the gonfalonier an appointment for life, instead of
for the original paltry two months. While it is undeniable that
the government was considerably steadied by this measure, it
was not thereby relieved of the terrible yoke laid on it from the
year 1494 onward, as indeed on every state of the peninsula, by
reason of Italy's having become the fiercely disputed bone of
contention between France, the first invader, and Spain, the
prompt and relentless challenger of that invasion.

No more than with the detailed history of the renewed Florentine republic is it the business of this book to occupy itself
with the detailed history of the struggle between the two rival
powers of France and Spain for the domination of Italy. Its
business is with the Medici, with just sufficient attention given
the local Florentine and the general Italian developments to clear
the way to an understanding of the return of the Medici to
Florence in the year 1512. The capital point to grasp and never
again let go is that when King Charles of France conquered the
kingdom of Naples in 1494 and King Ferdinand of Spain pro-
tested and promptly nullified that conquest, a conflict was inaugurated between these two giant powers which so completely
reduced the small Italian states to insignificance that their only

chance of survival was to align themselves with the victor.
But not until half a century had elapsed or, to be precise, not
until the treaty of Cateau-Cambrésis of 1559 was it finally settled that the victory would fall to Spain. Consequently, for a
period of about sixty years the panicky local governments perpetually fluctuated in their choice between France and Spain,
and, their native land, become the battlefield of the two contending monarchies, was so constantly and cruelly ravaged that
in the course of the two generations the struggle lasted, it experienced not only a grinding material deterioration but also the
slow draining of the amazing spiritual energy that had been the
source of its unrivaled cultural achievements. Although it will
be only the occasional general event bearing directly on the
fortunes of the Medici that in these pages will be detached from
the complicated story of the interminable Franco-Spanish conflict, it is indispensable for the reader to keep the monstrously
entangled world situation on which the Medicean fortunes hung
constantly in mind.

And now, focusing narrowly on the Florentine republic during its brief eighteen-year duration, we encounter two towering
figures whose fame leaped the Tuscan boundaries and spread to
all the countries of Europe. One is Girolamo Savonarola, the
other Niccolò Machiavelli. It was none other than the prior of
San Marco who was chiefly responsible for the quick solution
of the crisis precipitated by the expulsion of the Medici, and to
him also more than to any other single sponsor of the reborn
republic was due the novel constitutional feature of the Grand
Council. It was the broadly representative Grand Council that
was counted on to provide an effective guarantee against the
return of the former tyrants, more especially as the overwhelming majority of its membership was made up of devoted, anti-
Medicean followers of the Dominican friar. What chiefly bound
them to their leader was his prophetic fervor coupled with the
fanatic zeal with which he declared himself sent by Heaven to
effect his constantly reiterated double purpose: the reform of

the church and the reform of the morals of the Florentines. But as he also never wavered in attributing the existing corruption in church and society to the Medicean regime, it followed that the strongest assurance against a future reaction favorable to the Medici was the prophet's continued domination of the city.

That apparently so necessary domination lasted a little less than four years, coming to a tragic close with the unforgettable spectacle of Savonarola's death at the stake on the great public square before the palace of the signory. The prophet came to his end in consequence of a plot spun between Pope Alexander VI at Rome and certain leading families of Florence, a group of optimates who from the first had been bitterly hostile to the friar's uncompromising teachings. But the plot could not have been successful, had not the plotters been able to draw the considerable contingent of the lukewarm among the friar's following over to their side. It is certain that, except for a tight band of stalwarts who never ceased devotedly to cherish the memory of Savonarola long after he was gone, the Florentines in the main applauded his overthrow. However, it is also certain that while in his person there vanished from the scene the most unbending of the opponents of the Medici, the exiled family gained no more than an indirect advantage from his downfall, since its enemies were still too numerous and too infuriated against it for its relatively few local supporters to venture again into the open.

The republic continued therefore to thread its timorous way among the perils of the general situation. Then, in the year 1502, it took that measure toward strengthening its executive which consisted in conferring on the gonfalonier of Justice an appointment for life. The citizen thus honored was Piero Soderini and, without even remotely suspecting it at the time, Soderini honored himself by accepting as his leading adviser a man employed in the relatively unimportant position of chief of a service called the second chancellery. His name was Niccolò Machiavelli and, although he was never elevated to a higher post in the political hierarchy, he so greatly impressed Soderini with his exceptional command of both the domestic and the foreign fields that the gonfalonier drew him into consultation in all matters of policy, thus enabling him to exercise a political influence second only to that of the gonfalonier himself.

In his capacity of Soderini's leading consultant Machiavelli scored one qualified success and suffered one unqualified defeat. Even the success came to nothing in the end for the unanswerable reason that the Florentines were not ready for the sacrifices it imposed. Heartsick, like his countrymen without exception, over the intolerable military system of hired mercenaries, he came to the conclusion that it had imperatively to be replaced with a citizen army adequately trained in peacetime and closely bound together under the strain of war by the sentiment of patriotism. For so many centuries had the Florentines by the time of the revived republic been disused to arms that at the first whisper of Machiavelli's project it was buried under a wave of hostility and scorn. Stubbornly refusing to be deflected from his purpose, he gradually wrung permission from the Grand Council to go ahead experimentally and after a few years had the satisfaction of seeing a national militia slowly beginning to take shape. Unfortunately, before it had reached the consolidation to which its sponsor aspired, it was put to the test of confronting in the field the Spanish infantry, which was the supreme professional formation of its kind to be found at that time in Europe, and before this veteran body the Florentine novices dissolved like snow before a torrid blast. Poor Machiavelli experienced the greatest disappointment of his life; but by every fair consideration of his projected institution he deserves to be incorporated among the enlightened forerunners who through the ages have advocated a reform which was written in the stars but for which contemporary opinion was not yet ready.

The one unmitigated defeat Machiavelli suffered occurred in connection with the policy adopted to preserve the republic in the face of a new Franco-Spanish crisis. On the occasion in question the crisis originated neither with France nor Spain but with one of the most famous in the long succession of papal incumbents, Julius II. There was a certain grandeur about this pope which has won him a place among the towering figures of the Renaissance. Yielding to the attraction kind feels for kind, he drew into his employ the leading artists of his time and gained the respect and gratitude of all the succeeding generations of men by putting Michelangelo to work on the Sistine ceiling and Raphael on the *stanze* of the Vatican.

As in the case of all the popes of the period, the religious vein was far less strongly developed in Julius II than the secular vein, which consistently directed his activity. Consequently, he was not held back by religious scruples from plunging impulsively into the contest for supremacy between France and Spain and from developing in the course of the merely selfish pursuit of his advantage the ambitious plan of liberating the peninsula from both of its tormentors. It was in the year 1510 that he raised the war-cry, "Fuori i Barbari" (Put the barbarians out!), and invited the many small Italian states to join him in a common national effort, directed, however, for the present against France alone. It need hardly be pointed out that the slight flaw in the program was that it was based on something that did not exist, on an Italian national sentiment.

Florence was only one of several Italian states which bluntly declined to act on the pope's plea. It followed that the campaign against King Louis XII of France, who in 1498 had succeeded Charles VIII, was so feebly waged that it came to nothing. In his impotence and rage the pope now turned to Spain for help, thus resorting to the hazardous game of calling on the devil to cast out Beelzebub. The Spaniards, nothing loath, sent an army to the aid of the pope from Naples, which they had recently got firmly into their possession. Thereupon, in the year 1512, France and Spain engaged in a campaign plainly not, according to the pope's original purpose, to rid Italy of their presence, but rather to determine to which of them Italy was to fall as prize.

In April, 1512, a desperate battle was fought between the armies of the two invaders near Ravenna. It was finally won by the French. But it brought them no advantage, for, owing to their need of provisions, they were obliged to retreat northward toward their base at Milan, which, when the quarreling generals were unable to agree on a plan of campaign, they were constrained to abandon. Withdrawing more and more precipitately, they ended with giving up Italy altogether.

Before taking up the consequence for Florence of the abandonment of Italy by the defeated French, we shall have to give attention to the policy adopted by its republican government when in the year 1511 the pope's ideally conceived national union for the liberation of the peninsula took the irrational and self-defeating form of an appeal to the Spaniards to drive out the French. In his characteristically headlong manner, Julius II summoned Florence to join the revised national enterprise, which was manifestly no longer national, and curtly demanded an immediate acceptance. For many past generations the Florentines had been in the habit of looking on themselves as the beneficiaries and clients of mighty France and not even their recent betrayal at the hands of Charles VIII had weakened their traditional attachment. Since it was their inalterable conviction that this protector of theirs, this France, would always in the end top the heap, they were persuaded that in the newest phase of the Franco-Spanish struggle inaugurated in 1512, it was the French who would ultimately carry the field. So fierce and unanimous was the pro-Gallic sentiment of Gonfalonier Soderini's countrymen that it swept him off his feet like them and moved him quickly and categorically to reject the papal summons.

It was over this issue that Machiavelli suffered his one capital defeat as the leading adviser of the head of the state. Alone among his infatuated compatriots, he implored Soderini to await developments before committing himself in the impending conflict. Against what to the obsessed gonfalonier and citizens appeared as the inescapable obligation of loyalty, he advocated the more immediately pressing obligation of self-preservation. This in his eyes should always and everywhere be a government's primary consideration, and undebatably so in an instance like the present one, in which a minor power was asked to choose between two major powers, each exclusively motivated by naked self-interest.

Again we are tempted to exclaim "Poor Machiavelli," for he fared like a man attempting to stop a stampede of runaway horses. However, not even his exceptional political genius could be expected to have foreseen the complete evacuation of Italy which the French carried out in the summer of 1512 and by which they delivered their Florentine ally to the vengeance of its enemies. On assembling in congress at Mantua the victors agreed without a dissenting voice that the city's republican government would have either to surrender at discretion or be removed by force. But how was it to be replaced? No debate took place at Mantua or was required, for the answer to the question was at hand in the person of Cardinal Giovanni de' Medici, who presided over the congress of victors as the representative of the pope. As from a court of solemn, black-robed judges fell the unanimous verdict that the republic was to be replaced by the restoration of the former rulers.

Driven from Florence eighteen years before, the three sons of the Magnificent Lorenzo had experienced the usual mixed fortunes which in view of the restoration decreed at Mantua it behooves us briefly to examine. It is certain that the turbulent Piero II had learned nothing from his overthrow and that he conducted himself in exile in the same headstrong and violent manner as during his short reign. His foolish fixed purpose was to recover his lost authority by a successful military lunge against the city of his fathers, and more than once he actually led a band of hireling troops to the gates of Florence with the idea of inciting by his action a rising of his local partisans. His attempts failed miserably without curing him of his childish persuasion that force was a better counselor than moderation. In one of the innumerable campaigns between France and Spain he joined the French army and in the course of the hasty retreat of the French following a smashing Spanish victory was drowned in the waters of the swift Garigliano. In this manner the self-infatuated and unlamented Piero came to his end in the year 1503.

If we are justified in thinking of him as more of a feudal Orsini than an urban Medici in his total disposition, his younger brothers, Cardinal Giovanni and Giuliano, though very different one from the other, prevailingly exhibited what are plainly recognizable as Medicean traits. Both were definitely civil characters, averse to violence, and of a humane and gracious temper. Giuliano, inclined to softness and self-indulgence, became as he grew up a cultivated aristocrat, so deficient in energy and ambition that the outstanding member of the fraternal trio, Cardinal Giovanni, found it necessary after a number of vain attempts to turn him to political account, to leave him to the undisturbed pursuit of his pleasures.

It thus came about that the restoration of the Medicean fortunes hung solely on Lorenzo's second son and, although he was well endowed in several directions, we may categorically affirm that neither he nor his family would ever again have figured in Florentine affairs had it not been for Lorenzo's foresight in providing for young Giovanni's elevation to the college of cardinals. This made him a prince of the church with a palace at Rome and sufficient returns from ecclesiastical benefices to cut a distinguished figure in the capital of the Christian world. As soon as, on the death of Piero, he became the head of the house, he made a clean break with his older brother's violent policy whereby the ancient Florentine aversion to the Medici had been transformed into flaming hatred. The cardinal at once made it clear that there would be no more attempts to regain Florence by force of arms. At the same time he underscored his

altered attitude by graciously entertaining every Florentine visitor of Rome regardless of his party affiliation.

While the improved atmosphere he achieved did the cardinal
credit, it cannot be pretended that it figured importantly in the
restoration of his family to Florence which he achieved. That
event came about by his signalizing himself as a highly competent member of the college of cardinals coupled with the ever
erratic and incalculable fluctuations on the Italian political
scene. It was the familiar story of a man of parts confronting
a shifting situation which he was then able to manipulate to
his advantage. When Pope Julius II took up his novel national
policy, he discovered in Cardinal Medici his most sympathetic
and capable assistant. It was on this account that he appointed
him, on the occasion of the crucial campaign of 1512, as his
personal representative with the allied Spanish army.

The Spanish victory that followed was therefore in a sense
the cardinal's own victory and secured him a leading role in the
resulting congress of Mantua. No sooner had this body assembled than it called the recalcitrant Florentine government to
judgment. Its sentence, as we have just heard, ran to the effect
that the city must free itself of its guilty government and agree
to the return of the Medici. When Gonfalonier Soderini, ardently
backed by the whole population, spurned these humiliating
terms, the congress ordered the triumphant Spanish army to
cross the Apennines and enforce the will of the victors by military might.

Toward the end of August at Prato, hardly more than ten
miles from the Tuscan capital, the Florentine militia of Machiavelli's creation encountered the advancing Spaniards. The young
and relatively untrained national forces broke at the first assault
and scattered in wild flight in every direction. On news of the
disaster reaching Florence it produced a panic culminating in a
sudden revulsion of sentiment. Gonfalonier Soderini sought
safety in flight and a commission was dispatched post-haste to
Prato to wring the best obtainable terms from the victorious

Spanish general. The gist of the settlement it achieved was the payment of their expenses to the Spaniards and the humble acceptance of the once haughtily rejected demand of the restoration of the Medici.

Thereupon the brothers, first Giuliano and, a few days later, the cardinal, entered the city, the latter with all the pomp appropriate to his ecclesiastical dignity. According to the Prato terms the re-impatriated Medici were to have no higher status than that of private citizens. Undeniably, however, they had been brought back by Spanish bayonets and were protected in the city by mercenaries in their own pay whom they had quietly smuggled into the palace and piazza. In these circumstances could it even for a moment be pretended that they were citizens on an equal footing with the rest of the Florentines?

XII

THE RULE OF POPE LEO X

THE question of the civil status of the restored family was
settled with a minimum of delay. The ceremonial entrance
of Cardinal Giovanni into the city occurred on September 14.
Two days later he abolished the existing constitution and replaced it with its Medicean predecessor. The agency he employed to effect this *coup d'état* was the parliament which, because it had served as the tricky device underlying the Medicean
rule, had been formally outlawed on the family's expulsion in
1494. The cardinal and his local adherents, who had at once
gathered about him in close defensive formation, could think
of no better way of imposing their rule on their countrymen
than by restoring the former abominated instrument of tyranny.

In calling the parliament from the grave the procedure under
which it had operated in the past was closely followed: Only
Medicean partisans were admitted to the piazza; they shouted a
vociferous approval of the proposed balìa of Medicean nominees;
and the balìa wasted no time in going about the business for
which it was appointed. After abolishing in express terms all
the distinctive institutions of the recent regime, such as the
Grand Council and Machiavelli's national militia, it ordered a

return to the traditional signory of eight priors and a gonfalonier of Justice serving a short two-month term. A single departure from the earlier Medicean practice was that the balìa was never again discharged. It remained in power, nominated the successive signories, and directed and controlled their policy. Its permanence seemed to make it the final authority in the state. This, however, was not the case, for it took its orders by private channels from the cardinal. Consequently, the cardinal, as topping the reconstructed government, was its secret—and yet not so very secret—lord and master.

The mild spirit of the cardinal was displayed in his refusal to inaugurate his rule with the all too usual arrest and execution of his leading political opponents. Owing, however, to his natural distrust of them, he did gradually ease them out of office, replacing them with dependable Medicean partisans. The most distinguished victim of this policy was Niccolò Machiavelli. So little was he a doctrinaire republican that he would without any doubt have faithfully served the restored Medici in return for the retention of his secretarial post. His dismissal dealt him a crushing blow, for, in all likelihood, not since the world began has there been a man more wrapped up in the state *per se* and more bent on discovering the procedures and measures that promote or hamper its well-being. Life to Niccolò was politics and outside of politics there was no life. Only reluctantly did he persuade himself that his days of office-holding were over. Well, then, if an angel with a flaming sword stood between him and a career of practical politics, he would become a closet-politician and give himself to the theoretic study of the state. It was a decision by which he won a place among the immortal authors in this field in the long succession of the ages. Among his leading productions are the *Discourses on the First Ten Books of Livy* and the epigrammatically compressed study called *The Prince*. A particular merit of the latter work is its grim and unrivaled portrait of that form of government, the tyranny, which in Machiavelli's day was making its triumphal march through Italy and Europe.

Six months after the cardinal's assumption of the Florentine government he experienced a change of status, the importance of which cannot be exaggerated: in March, 1513, being at the time but thirty-seven years old, he was elected pope in succession to the stormy petrel of recent Italian politics, Julius II. His fellow citizens, regardless of their political coloring, received the news with wild demonstrations of joy, so greatly did it flatter their pride that a Florentine had achieved the highest honor of Christendom. The popular excitement received additional stimulation from the hunger aroused among numerous individual Florentines for the favors a friendly, tiara-crowned pope was able to dispense.

On mounting the papal throne the cardinal adopted the title of Leo X. Universally regarded as the embodiment of the culture of the age, he readily conformed to the general expectation by promptly coming forward as the friend of the humanists and patron of the artists. He is said to have disclosed his worldly frame of mind by an astounding statement to his intimates on the day of his election. It was: "Now that God has given us the papacy, let us enjoy it." While the saying may be legendary, as such apposite sayings generally are, it nonetheless is an accurate, summary reflection of his essential attitude. Innumerable scholars, poets, musicians, architects, and painters, who rushed to Rome at his accession, found employment at his hands. Although they were in the main a vulgar horde of mediocrities and sychophants, it will always be gratefully remembered that, included in his patronage, were also the two greatest artists of the day, Raphael and Michelangelo.

An act of Julius II, to which this pope in large measure owes his good repute among later generations, is that it was he who first drew Raphael and Michelangelo to Rome and set them to work on truly majestic commissions. This support Leo X was inclined to continue, but what a difference in the work each artist did for the two patrons! It is worth while to have a glance at this difference both for its own sake and for the sake of the light it throws on the quality and character respectively of Julius and Leo. Some native flair of Julius for grandeur, an objective grandeur, be it observed, completely dissociated from narrow personal ends, prompted him to propose to the two masters he had drawn into his service commensurate commissions, by which each found his creative powers stimulated to their highest potency. It was at Julius's behest that Raphael painted in a room or *stanza* of the Vatican the greatest group of allegorical projections of the essential elements of Western culture that has ever seen the light and that Michelangelo limned on the ceiling of the Sistine chapel his noble and unrivaled story of creation. These two works mark the summit of achievement for their respective authors; and it does not remotely detract from their glory to assert that their genius would not have climbed to this height without the relentless pressure of the genius of the great Julius.

At the death of Julius, Raphael was working at a second Vatican stanza devoted to the pictured presentation of selected miracles of the Christian story, and this group of wall paintings, though of entirely different inspiration than the allegories of the first stanza, shows no falling off of the specific Raphaelesque magic. But the next or third stanza, which was commissioned by Leo X, records a precipitous decline. For some reason that can no longer be recovered Raphael reduced his connection with the work on this stanza to a general supervision and left the details of execution to, in some instances, painfully dull and mediocre apprentices. True, Pope Leo found other and fairly adequate employment for Raphael in the open galleries surrounding one of the Vatican courts. Here the master did along the vaulted ceiling a series of notable paintings dealing with the Bible story. Their smaller scale and diminished significance may be taken as an accurate reflection of the difference in mental and moral stature between the far-ranging, lordly Julius and his self-indulgent, pleasure-loving successor.

In the case of Michelangelo, Leo went even farther astray. With his self-centered passion for the exaltation of his family he turned Michelangelo, who by decree of nature was a sculptor and who by decree of Pope Julius and against his own stubborn will had become a painter, into an equally unwilling architect. Leo took this course because he wished to point Michelangelo's creative gift to the glorification of his house. The church of San Lorenzo, erected by Brunelleschi at the behest of Cosimo more than half a century before, still stared at the passers-by with a blank face, since it had never been provided with a façade. This defect Leo resolved to remedy by ordering the missing frontispiece from the greatest living Florentine artist. The consequence was a comedy or, more truly, a somber tragedy of errors which cannot be recounted here. Suffice it that the façade was never built and that the failure to put Michelangelo's talents to suitable use in Pope Leo's time must unflinchingly be laid at this pontiff's door.

Mixed with Leo's native endowment of energy and will, without which he would never have mounted the papal throne, there had been in him from birth a soft, hedonistic strain, to which, with the satisfaction of his highest ambition, he increasingly succumbed with the consequent inevitable deterioration of his moral and mental fiber. An examination of the famous portrait Raphael did of him reveals the man in his later papal phase more unerringly than the most searching words. The Leo of this canvas is a large, flabby man, whose native energy and refined taste have been all but destroyed by too exclusive association with flatterers and buffoons and by habitual self-indulgence.

If the business of this book were with the Roman curia, this would be the place to take up Leo's conduct of the papacy. We should then discover, had it not been unforgettably brought home to us in our earliest school years as the overshadowing fact of his reign, that it was during his incumbency that the Protestant revolt began and that, forced with the utmost reluctance on his part to face it, he proved himself the fatally inadequate

helmsman of the storm-tossed ship of the church. His cultivated, worldly outlook, no longer touched with even a lingering
religious tinge, rendered him incapable of understanding the
moral fervor that inspired the movement of protest inaugurated
by Martin Luther. He smiled scornfully at its earliest manifestations as beneath his notice, as, in his opinion, a mere squabble
of cantankerous monks, and when he could no longer ignore its
later cataclysmic developments, he never rose above the view
that the fateful agitation could be quieted by diplomatic legerdemain judiciously supplemented by the employment of brute
force. He conducted himself with hardly greater effectiveness
in regard to the continuing political struggle between France
and Spain for the domination of Italy. He shifted from Spain
to France and back again, and although by his nimble foot-work
he may have saved himself from immediate disaster, he sacrificed
every claim to the position of a self-reliant, independent political
agent.

Affirming once more that Leo's detailed conduct of the papal
office lies beyond our scope, still we are not dispensed from keeping it constantly in mind as we focus on the narrower fortunes
of his rule over his recovered Florentine dominion. On the day he
left Florence to attend the conclave from which he issued as
pope, he became an absentee ruler and was obliged to appoint a
substitute, who then in the eyes of the Florentines and the world
in general would make show as the responsible head of the state.
Of course the substitute would not be really responsible, for Leo
at Rome would not be so far away that he could not keep him
in leading-strings; but since it would serve the never negligible
cause of decent appearances if the local government would have,
or would seem to have, a responsible resident head, he acted on
that judgment. On first attacking the problem he gave consideration to his brother Giuliano as the resident head of the state
but quickly dismissed the thought, owing to Giuliano's long since
proved political incapacity. However, as his younger brother
possessed an undeniable personal allure, Leo continued to nurse

projects which, while elevating Giuliano in public esteem, would also serve the purpose ever present to the pope's mind of adding to the luster of the house of Medici.

With our attention drawn to Leo's concern for the advance of Giuliano, we may as well carry the story to its close, even though it breaks a desirable continuity. One way of measuring the gradual rise of the Medici in the world is the record of their marriages. From the early long succession of solid bourgeois marriages they passed with Lorenzo the Magnificent's Orsini bride into the aristocratic class. It remained for Pope Leo to envisage royalty as the family's proper goal and in this matter to be content with no less an affiliation than with the oldest royalty of Europe, the royalty of France. In the year 1515 he used a favorable political conjunction to obtain the consent of young King Francis I of France to the marriage of a princess related to his house to the attractive but feckless Giuliano. Included in the bargain was the elevation of the bridegroom to a French title. Accordingly, he was formally named duke of Nemours, but already long since wasting away with tuberculosis, he died a year after the exchange of the marriage vows. His early death did not cancel the memorable change effected in the status of the Medici. They ranked henceforth as royalty and never again did a male member of the house contract a marriage on a lower social level.

It is highly probable that Leo never thought seriously of any other member of his house as the Florentine substitute for himself than the misguided Piero II's son. This son, Lorenzo by name, was a handsome, vigorous youth twenty years of age on the return of his family from exile. By the principle of succession to which the Medici had adhered from the days of Cosimo he was the heir presumptive, and Pope Leo would probably have established him in office without delay, had he not wished to keep him under observation for a while to see how far he had inherited the arrogant disposition of his father. On taking up residence at Rome, Leo no longer hesitated and not without a lingering measure of reserve installed the young man in the seat of power. His continuing reserve was manifested by his frequent dispatch of counsel to his young nephew and by requiring him to accept as his secretary an official of Leo's choice charged with making a day by day report to Rome on Lorenzo's conduct of office. If Lorenzo reigned at Florence, it was still the pope at Rome who ruled.

Besides the civil rule of Florence, Leo exercised also the civil rule of the papal state. This by the time of his accession had achieved a greatly improved consolidation by the action begun by Sixtus IV and continued more or less consistently by his successors. By far the most vigorous promoter of territorial consolidation had been Leo X's immediate predecessor, Julius II, for it was he who had turned the startlingly successful unifying labors of the infamous Caesar Borgia to the advantage of the papacy. Everyone at all read in the history of the Italy of this period will recall that Caesar Borgia, son of Pope Alexander VI and ruthless pinnacle of the century-old plague of condottiere outlaws, had put to the sword all the petty tyrants of the State of the Church who dared resist him. He had done so with the secret plan of turning his conquests to his own advantage by fusing them into a personal dominion. His scheme, fatal to the aspirations of the papacy, had been defeated by the premature death of his father and sponsor, Alexander VI, and the succession of Julius II, by whose resolute spirit Caesar Borgia had been driven out of Italy and the fruits of his crimes transferred to the papal account.

There can be no doubt that Leo X approved of the unifying policy of his predecessor, for he had, as cardinal, been actively employed in carrying it out. It is also beyond challenge that on being elevated to the papacy, he determined to follow in Julius II's footsteps. But it was not long before this high resolve clashed with his ambition at all costs to exalt his family and, more particularly, his nephew Lorenzo, the unofficial and untitled ruler of Florence. If it should be asked why in his desire to raise Lorenzo to a loftier dignity he did not put an end to the long since transparent fiction of the purely citizen rank of the Medici and make public disclosure of the actual situation by endowing Lorenzo with the title of duke of Florence, the answer is that Leo, as a born Florentine, had an intimate knowledge of the republican passion of his countrymen and prudently shrank from needlessly offending it.

But there were other ways of winning the coveted sovereign rank for Lorenzo. To this end Leo would have only to revert to the practice of innumerable papal predecessors and endow his nephew with some territory belonging to the church. True, by doing so not only would he be betraying the state intrusted to his care but he would be openly and shamefully revealing that he rated the fortunes of his family as of more account than his sworn obligation to the papal office. Nonetheless in the year 1516 he took the fatal step and, declaring the duke of the small mountain state of Urbino deposed, conferred his duchy on Lorenzo. Had he been prompted to remove the reigning duke in pursuit of the enlightened policy of territorial consolidation, it would not have been difficult to defend his action; but since he was motivated by no nobler purpose than the replacement of one usurping ruler by another closer to his heart, he was guilty of an infamy by which he has irretrievably besmirched his good name.

The installation of Lorenzo as duke of Urbino turned out to be much more difficult than Pope Leo had imagined. The deposed duke was a man of spirit and defended himself with blazing resolution. Consequently, Leo was put to the expense of recruiting an army, which was obliged to conduct an arduous winter campaign in one of the roughest regions of the Apennines. The pope's unscrupulous action made him many enemies who elatedly proclaimed it but a just retribution when Lorenzo, who had served as commander-in-chief of the papal forces, contracted an illness in the bitter climate of Urbino which permanently undermined his hitherto excellent health. For the moment, however, both Leo and Lorenzo might rest satisfied, for not only had Lorenzo become duke of Urbino but, on returning to Florence, where he officially ranked as a simple citizen, he was henceforth, out of a courtesy unworthy of a genuine republic, addressed by his ducal title.

But that was not the end of Leo's sleepless scheming in behalf of his nephew. Since through the marriage of his brother Giuliano the Medici had become connected with the reigning house of Valois, it was imperative that the advantage thus gained should be fortified by having young Lorenzo contract an equally exalted marriage. Leo therefore pursued this plan until he succeeded in persuading King Francis I to consent to the union of the new-fledged duke of Urbino with the young and beautiful French princess, Maddalena. The marriage took place in 1518. But again a shadow fell on the papal project, this time the black and final shadow; for in the year following the wedding the duchess died in childbed and was followed a month later by her husband, whose health had never recovered from its impairment dating from the grueling Urbino campaign. The child, to whom the duchess gave birth, survived her parents and in due time became a famous personage in French history who, under the name of Catherine de' Medici, played a leading role as the wife of one king and mother of his three successors. Although she does not figure in the history of Florence, she deserves mention in a work dealing with the older Medicean line as its last survivor, whom subtle human plotting supplemented by favoring turns of fortune raised to the highest worldly dignity any member of the family ever attained.

Keen was Pope Leo's grief over the passing of Lorenzo and not only for his nephew's sake. There was now no male left to perpetuate the Medici succession and to gain time for the consideration of the problem the absentee ruler of Florence sent thither as his representative his cousin, Cardinal Giulio de' Medici. Giulio was the illegitimate son of the handsome Giuliano, who on the occasion of the infamous Pazzi conspiracy had poured out his lifeblood before the high altar of the cathedral from twenty-nine dagger thrusts by his two ferocious attackers. Born in the year of his father's death, he had been adopted into the family by Lorenzo the Magnificent and given the same careful education as his own sons. The Magnificent pointed him toward a clerical career, and since nature had happily endowed the lad with his father's intelligence and courtesy, he rose rapidly in his chosen profession. No sooner had his cousin Leo mounted the papal throne than, with the advance of his family ever in mind, he made Giulio a cardinal and found in him so informed and trustworthy a counselor that he ended by unloading a large part of the burdens of office on the shoulders of his relative. Small wonder, then, that on the creation of the grave Florentine succession issue Leo should have dispatched Cardinal Giulio to the Arno as interim ruler.

Reliable evidence permits us confidently to affirm that Cardinal Giulio made a success of his critical mission. He avoided the lordly airs by which young Lorenzo, on acquiring the ducal title, had latterly given offense and, remembering that Florence was still officially a republic, he made a point of regularly calling groups of citizens into conference on current municipal business. Further, his living in simple burgher style in the family mansion made a good impression, and highly satisfactory, especially to the owners of property, was his prudent management of the public finances. In sum, Cardinal Giulio measurably increased the Medici prestige during his interim rule.

In the very year of Lorenzo's death and Cardinal Giulio's taking over the Florentine succession another stage had been reached in the interminable Franco-Spanish struggle over Italy. It was inaugurated by the death in January, 1519, of Emperor Maximilian and the heated German election contest that followed. The choice of the electors fell at last on the king of Spain. This was Charles, a youth of nineteen, who had entered on the rule of Spain three years before on the demise of his maternal grandfather, the capable and grasping King Ferdinand. However,

Charles did not owe his winning of the imperial prize to his being the king of Spain. He owed it to the fact that his father, Philip, who died young, was the son of Emperor Maximilian, head of the house of Hapsburg and archduke of the leading German principality of Austria.[1] It was because Philip had married Joan, daughter of Ferdinand and Isabella and heiress of Spain that their oldest son, Charles, reached the throne of Spain and ultimately brought the enormous possessions of the lines of both father and mother into his single hand. While at the time of Emperor Maximilian's death young Charles was already king of Spain, king of Naples, and lord of the Netherlands, what weighed with the German electors was not so much this multiple grandeur as his being also a German prince, specifically an Austrian archduke, and he won the German election owing solely to this circumstance.

In the year 1520 young Charles, fifth of the name, came to Germany to be crowned emperor and incidentally to look into the revolt against the Catholic church inaugurated three years before by Martin Luther. The care-free Leo X had at last been sufficiently aroused to excommunicate Luther and now demanded that the newly elected emperor do his part by bringing the declared heretic to his trial and death. As a convinced Catholic believer, Charles was disposed to meet the pope's demand but, on arriving in Germany, he encountered so powerful a current of opinion favorable to Luther that he resolved to refer the issue to the meeting of the German princes, called the Reichstag. Summoned before this assembly, which met at the city of Worms on the Rhine, Luther courageously repeated his earlier attacks on the church and closed with a ringing refusal to withdraw them unless disproved by Holy Writ.

It meant a deadlock, which Charles V, wise beyond his years

[1] *Genealogical Table of the House of Hapsburg:*
Emperor Maximilian I (1493-1519) archduke of Austria, m. Mary, heiress of Burgundy and the Netherlands
Philip the Handsome (d. 1506) m. Joan, daughter of Ferdinand of Aragon and Isabella of Castile, and heiress of Spain
Emperor Charles V (1519-1556)

in the ways of diplomacy, resolved to break by a secret treaty with Leo X. In this document of May, 1521, he agreed to the desired civil condemnation of Luther but not without a suitable *quid pro quo*. The reader will recall that some nine years before, in 1512, the Spaniards with the aid of Pope Julius II, had driven the French out of Italy. But the French refused to accept their defeat as final and in 1515, on the accession to the throne of the young and warlike Francis I, had returned to the attack and by a brilliant victory at Marignano had again got possession of the crucial duchy of Milan. Shortly after, the sixteen-year-old Charles became king of Spain and determined, as soon as the favorable occasion should turn up, again to drive the French out of the Milanese vantage-point and to resume the domination of the Italian peninsula throughout its length. The favorable occasion turned up at Worms following the dead-locked session of the Reichstag over the case of Martin Luther. In return for the pope's joining in a renewed effort to eject the French from Milan, Charles V agreed to close the Reichstag meeting with the solemn condemnation of the culprit before the bar, the excommunicated Augustinian friar, Martin Luther.

The new war between France and Spain began at once and led to still another of the dramatic reversals which had marked the struggle of the two powers over Italy from the beginning. Merely by clever maneuvering and without the usual climax of a pitched battle, the Imperialists, as the many kinds of troops in the employ of Charles V were henceforth called, forced the French to abandon Milan and retreat in full dissolution toward the passes of the Alps. When the news reached Rome, Pope Leo ordered a general celebration. At this, extended far into a November night, he was seized with chills and fever. He had never possessed great physical stamina and had recently been subjected to a dangerous operation for the removal of an anal ulcer. In spite of his youth, for he was only forty-six years old, he could not shake off the sharp bronchitis that followed his chills and died after three days on December 1, 1521.

THE RULE OF POPE CLEMENT VII INCLUDING
THE REPUBLICAN INTERLUDE OF 1527-1530

THE death of Pope Leo X did not interrupt Cardinal Giulio
de' Medici's rule of the Florentine state. In spite of occasional duty visits to Rome, he continued to make Florence his
residence, occupying himself to the best of his ability and with
considerable success with the routine business of government.
But his problem of problems, ever present in the back of his
head, was how to replace his purely interim rule with an establishment of a more permanent and, at the same time, of a continued Medicean character. However, as to these two, to his
mind, inseparable demands he was faced with an insurmount-
able difficulty: he, priest and cardinal, was the last male of his
line. There were, to be sure, some women of his stock available,
there was, above all, the little Catherine born in 1519; but he
refused to consider women, since they had never figured in the
family succession. Not that there were not, as he was acutely
aware, certain Medici males dwelling within the compass of the
city. They belonged to the younger branch of the house, which
boasted the elder Cosimo's younger brother, Lorenzo, as its

founder. But the two lines had quarreled and, like Leo X before him, Cardinal Giulio did not view the younger branch as other than a house of strangers.

Cardinal Giulio was still pondering the knotty question of the succession when an event at Rome fundamentally altered the situation. Following the death of Leo X, the conclave, which met in the year 1522, had elected to the papacy an ascetic, medieval-minded north-European of Flemish nationality who took the title of Hadrian VI. Completely out of tune with Renaissance Italy, this austere foreigner on arriving in Italy promptly aroused the hatred and, what was even worse, the scorn and ridicule of the luxurious papal court. A conflict brewed which ended before it was well started with the death of Hadrian barely a year after his election. Instinctively the ensuing conclave of the year 1523 undertook to correct its recent error by choosing as Hadrian's successor not only a native Italian but an Italian unmistakably congenial to the ruling Roman atmosphere. With these lively nativist sentiments no one stood in closer accord than Cardinal Giulio de' Medici. On issuing triumphantly from the election he assumed the tiara under the title of Clement VII.

In view of his excellent administrative record under Leo X at both Rome and Florence, Clement's accession to the papacy was received with universal satisfaction. Never were apparently justified expectations more crushingly disappointed; for Clement in the course of his eleven-year rule was overwhelmed with such a succession of calamities as to make his reign one of the most disastrous in the long history of his office. Without doubt these calamities were in large part the mere mounting to a peak of difficulties, such, for instance, as the Protestant revolt, which had been gathering momentum for generations past and for which his predecessors rather than himself were responsible. The defense is equally pertinent to the struggle for the domination of Italy between France and Spain, two mighty military powers by which the militarily feeble pope was threatened with being ground to bits as between millstones. At Clement's accession to the papacy the Franco-Spanish conflict had already been going on for over a quarter of a century, throughout which time the leading concern of his predecessors had necessarily been first, to escape an ever threatening destruction, and second, as far as may be, to maintain their ancient claim to an unquestioned sovereign status in their Italian territories.

With every allowance made for the existence of religious and political pressures of enormous power antedating his accession, it is indisputable that the conspicuous failure of Pope Clement to steer his course successfully among these hazards was at least due in part to certain defects of character and, primarily, to a fatal flaw of indecision. The flaw had probably always been present but had not made itself strongly felt as long as its owner was occupied with the strictly administrative labors intrusted to him by his cousin Leo. However, with the assumption of full executive responsibility, it came disastrously into play. We shall not trace his perpetual fluctuations over the ever more menacing religious revolt of northern Europe, since the Protestant movement is manifestly outside our province; we shall not even exhibit his hazardous oscillation between the two invading powers of Italy beyond what is strictly necessary for the comprehension of contemporary events at Florence. But since the Florentine events constitute a unique climax both of the ancient passion of the citizens for a free commonwealth and of the urge of the Medici dating from old Cosimo to make their rule permanent, and since, further, it was the fatal plunge of Clement into the Franco-Spanish rivalry that produced the ever memorable Florentine political rising of 1527, we are inescapably obliged to unfold the pope's role in the contemporary power game and to follow it through to its tragic consequences.

Clement VII's political catastrophe may be traced back to that renewal by Emperor Charles V of his struggle with France which was inaugurated by his treaty with Pope Leo X in 1521 and by which, in return for the condemnation of Luther, he received Leo's support in the projected war against Francis I.

In the previous chapter we took account of the upset effected in northern Italy by the quick success of the fresh struggle against the French and recorded its fateful aftermath for Leo X by reason of his exposing himself to the night chill while celebrating the victory of his ally. With the re-occupation by the Spaniards of Milan, their immediate objective, the war was by no means over, for Francis I clung to his Italian ambition and in the autumn of 1524 made another concentrated effort to realize it. Crossing the Alps with a magnificently equipped army, he descended into the Lombard plain. The Imperialists, outnumbered, sought safety in retreat, except for a small force of four thousand men who continued to garrison Pavia. To this city King Francis laid siege, but it defended itself so stubbornly that the Imperialists had time to assemble a relief army of Spanish and German troops. As it was contrary to King Francis' chivalrous code to retreat on vulgar considerations of safety, his besieging host was, on February 24, 1525, caught between the newly created Imperialist army and the Pavia garrison and virtually annihilated. Francis himself was captured and carried to Spain, the prisoner of his rival.

The blow of Pavia fell almost as heavily on Clement VII as on France and its king. Tied to Spain by Leo's treaty of 1521, the pope, lacking military power, had been obliged to serve the common cause with payments in cash and by the long continuation of these levies had been bled white by the exacting Spaniards. Consequently, he nursed the secret hope of a French success, moderate rather than sweeping but sufficient to establish a desirable balance of power between Spain and France, thereby winning back for him his lost and lamented independence. That hope was so completely blasted by Pavia that in his disillusioned eyes he was now himself no better than a prisoner of Charles V.

For the present there was nothing to do but patiently to await developments. They were not long in appearing. A year after his capture King Francis came to terms with his jailer and by the terms of the treaty of Madrid of March 18, 1526, regained his freedom in return for the surrender to Charles of all his Italian claims together with a number of other extremely humiliating commitments, which we need not consider because they were not carried out. Hardly back on French soil, the liberated French king cast his engagements to the winds and with a view to an early renewal of the war promptly opened negotiations with the pope and such other Italian states as resented the onerous and by now undisguised enslavement of their country to the Spanish monarch.

Pope Clement met the overtures of King Francis with passionate eagerness, although in the manner of the weak and timid he did his best to conceal from his overbearing ally, the emperor, that he was about to desert him. But Charles was not deceived by lying professions of continued devotion and revolved appropriate measures to keep Clement from throwing his weight into the French scales. It proved a considerable help that the French had gone ahead diplomatically before they were ready militarily, with the result that, in spite of lavish promises, no French army appeared on Italian soil. However, in the over-confident expectation of the early arrival of such an army the pope and his scattered Italian allies went ahead assembling the contingents which they were obligated to provide under their respective secret treaties with their French sponsor. Among the Italian allies of France was the city of Florence. Not that the people of Florence had of their own free will committed themselves to the new war, for ever since the return of the Medici in 1512 the government of the city had effectively rested, as our story has clearly demonstrated, with the two representatives of the house who successively became Popes Leo and Clement. It was therefore exclusively by the decision of Clement that a small Florentine force was in the winter of 1526-27 taken in pay. The idea was for it to co-operate with the contingents put in the field by Clement in his capacity of pope and by certain other Italian states and the designated purpose of these levies was to block any offensive action the Spaniards might see fit to undertake.

It was the good fortune of the poorly co-ordinated anti-imperialist allies that, owing to the chronic exhaustion of the Spanish treasury, the army which Charles maintained in Italy had by this same winter of 1526-27 been so greatly reduced that it had lost its striking power. However, pricked by the open preparations of their enemies, Charles's representatives in Italy resorted to emergency measures to re-invigorate their reduced forces and succeeded in assembling a few Spanish and German regiments in Lombardy. Then, to take advantage of the manifest confusion in the camp of their enemies they boldly ordered them to march southward toward Rome in the hope of bringing to terms their leading adversary, the pope, before the expected French army should have appeared on the scene. Since the Spaniards and Germans of this improvised army were ill-disposed to each other and since, besides, they were both in a mutinous frame of mind owing to steadily mounting arrears of pay, it would not have been difficult to stop them, had there been even a minimum measure of agreement among their opponents. But these opponents were agreed in nothing save in their will to disagree and by their flagrant inaction enabled the Imperialists to push unmolested down half the length of the peninsula and pitch camp on May 4 in the Tiber meadows outside the papal capital.

Two days later they breached the walls and, pouring into Rome like swollen waters over a broken dam, held the city at their mercy. Clement VII and his cardinals were just able to save their lives by taking refuge in the castle of Sant' Angelo, which defended the Vatican quarter. Around them raged such a sack as the Eternal City had not even experienced in the distant days of the fall of Roman civilization. Many of the German mercenaries were followers of Martin Luther and vented their hatred of Catholicism on the rich furnishings of the altars and on the persons of the great prelates whom they succeeded in capturing, while the Spaniards, who, on shaking off their accustomed discipline, were no better than wild beasts, roamed the town in search of the immense stores of gold, silver, jewels, and wealth of every kind which had been accumulated through the ages in the capital of the Christian world. The horrible orgy terminated only when the pope accepted the terms dictated by the victors and in pledge of their fulfillment agreed to remain a prisoner in the castle of Sant' Angelo at the discretion of the emperor.

Try as the historian may—and this historian has honestly tried—he will not be able to persuade himself to pass in silence over an episode of the siege which, relatively unimportant in itself, has been preserved for us in the incomparably racy speech of one of the outstanding figures of the period. I am referring to the Florentine silversmith, Benvenuto Cellini, who, held in high esteem in his own time for his excellence as a craftsman, owes his reputation among later generations not so much to his handiwork as to an autobiography he left behind than which there is no livelier and more revealing mirror of the age. Benvenuto happened to be at Rome at the time of the siege and volunteered to help defend the castle of Sant' Angelo, in which the pope and his court had taken refuge. It was owing to his being in his essential nature rather more of an adventurer and swashbuckler than a reflective artist that he was able to impart its incomparable flavor to the story of his life.

During the short two-day siege the pope passed much of his time on the ramparts of his castle of refuge and Benvenuto, who served among the defending gunners, was as usually sharply on the lookout to push himself to the front. Conspicuously tricked out in colorful attire there strutted among the besieging troops in the meadow below the battlements their commander-in-chief, the duke of Bourbon, a French prince, who in the not uncommon manner of the great lords of that day had deserted to the enemy. The other gunners having repeatedly trained their weapons at him and missed, it was now Benvenuto's turn. The pope encouraged him with a nod and even playfully laid a bet on him in evidence of his confidence in his Tuscan countryman. Taking careful aim, he brought the match to the fuse. There was a loud explosion followed by an even louder thunder of applause from the bystanders as Benvenuto's shot cleanly bifurcated the coxcomb duke by striking the very bull's-eye of the target, the invisible navel. Assuming the truth of the tale, which only a very pedantic mind would question, we are left wondering whether the gratified pope paid his bet to his sharp-shooting fellow townsman.

The news of the capture of Rome and the imprisonment of the pope precipitated events in Florence which fully to understand we shall have to look into the local developments that attended the transformation in 1523 of Cardinal Giulio de' Medici into Pope Clement VII. Obliged by his elevation to the papacy to make Rome his residence, he ended his long cogitations over the future rule of Florence by a decision that shook the citizens to the marrow of their bones. He disclosed the existence of two bastard Medici boys, of whom only the vaguest rumors had thus far been current, and dispatched them to Florence as its future rulers subject during their minority to the guardianship of Cardinal Passerini, who attended them in the capacity of the pope's personal representative.

There was a grave and disturbing uncertainty about the origin of the boys which, in spite of the curiosity they aroused at the time and have continued to arouse, has never been entirely cleared up. The reputedly older boy, Ippolito, was born in the year 1511 and was represented as being the illegitimate son of Giuliano, duke of Nemours, by an undisclosed woman of either Pesaro or Urbino. The other, Alessandro, born about the same time and possibly even a trifle older than Ippolito, was represented as the bastard son of Lorenzo, whom Pope Leo X had made duke of Urbino and who had actually ruled in Florence for a few years prior to his death in 1519. If Ippolito's birth was enveloped in uncertainty, Alessandro's has remained an impenetrable mystery. His villainous disposition coupled with his dusky skin, negroid lips, and crisp hair caused people to regard him as a monster and to put faith in the unsubstantiated rumor that his mother was a Moorish slave. Nor was that the worst of the whispers to which the secrecy wherein his origin was wrapped gave rise. Clement VII's manifest preference of the "monster" over the lively and extremely handsome Ippolito lent credence to the opinion, which recent investigators generally share, that, instead of his being the bastard son of Lorenzo, he was in point of fact the bastard son of the pope.

With a thickening stench of rumors enveloping the two dubious Medici offspring it need not be expressly stated that the Florentines regarded their presence among them with a mounting aversion which Cardinal Passerini's personal conduct did nothing to diminish. His open avarice invited disgust, his boorish manners contempt. With each day it became more evident that nothing save the power of the pope who, though residing at Rome, was the real ruler of the city, kept it from rising against his despicable agents. No wonder therefore the moment the unparalleled abasement suffered by Clement at the hands of the particolored bandits calling themselves soldiers was reported at Florence the citizens rose as of one accord to cast off his yoke. The frightened Passerini was obliged to recognize that even the semblance of a prop had suddenly vanished from under him. There was no violence to speak of, just a rising tide of irresistible opposition. Yielding to its pressure, on May 17, 1527, the cardinal evacuated the city carrying with him his two youthful Medici charges.

Songs of thanksgiving sounded through the streets as with the same unrestrained enthusiasm as in 1494 the Florentines celebrated the second ejection of their tyrants and reverted to the constitution under which they had lived during the earlier republican interlude. Its main feature, it will be recalled, was a democratic Grand Council which voted the laws and elected the signory of eight priors and their presiding officer, the gonfalonier of Justice. A departure, slight but not negligible, from the earlier practice was the reduction, owing to lingering fears of tyranny, of the gonfalonier's lifelong term of service to a single year. It must signally have gratified the ageing Machiavelli that his national militia, rejected by the restored Medici in 1512, was again taken into favor. He himself, it is true, was not restored to the secretarial post he so fully deserved, but his bitter disappointment was of short duration, for he died a month after the city's liberation.

For the time being the republican regime was not challenged from any quarter and, in point of fact, ran no risk of being challenged so long as Pope Clement remained the impotent prisoner of the emperor. Not until he had won his freedom would he be able to take up with any even remote chance of success what we may agree was his inalterable purpose: to bring his native city back again under the yoke of his house. The story of his reconciliation with Charles V is therefore not only pertinent but indispensable to our understanding of the fate of the renewed republic. Let the starting-point of our review of the incident be what we may call the political law which had been operative since the beginning of the Franco-Spanish conflict over Italy. It took the following simple form: if the relations between the pope and the king of France were good, those between him and the king of Spain were bad, and vice versa. Thus since it was the recent Franco-papal rapprochement that had reduced Clement VII to his present plight, his degradation was bound to continue until the pending war between Charles V and Francis I had been brought to another no matter how provisional a conclusion. Either the French promises of military intervention, which had failed to materialize in 1527, would be carried out in 1528 and the pope be restored to his honors by a victorious France, or France, registering another failure, would leave the pope so utterly helpless that, no longer able to defy the towering Charles, he would have unavoidably to come to a settlement with him.

Now, in the hope of making amends for his military defection in 1527 King Francis undertook to retrieve himself in the following year by dispatching a large and effective army into the Italian theater of war. He made the capable Lautrec its commander, and so vigorously did Lautrec press forward that the outnumbered Imperialists were obliged to avoid battle and to permit the French to push victoriously as far south as Naples. They then laid siege to this main Spanish base in the peninsula in the expectation with its capture to bring down in ruin the whole edifice of Spanish power in Italy. Only what for lack of a better understanding of human events we mortals call an act of God kept Lautrec from taking this key city on its storied bay. A ferocious pestilence, which broke out among the besieging host, in a matter of weeks reduced the French commander's proud army to a shrunken handful of completely dispirited troops. On the attempt of this remnant to save itself by retreat it was surrounded in the mountains by a superior Spanish force and obliged to surrender.

So complete was the disaster of 1528 that it eliminated France for a long time to come from Italian affairs and left Pope Clement no choice but to come to terms with Charles V. Fortunately, the emperor, whose Catholic conscience suffered keenly from the shame he had brought on the head of the church, was as eager as Clement to arrive at a settlement. Accordingly, negotiations were initiated which culminated in a treaty of peace and alliance signed at Barcelona on June 29, 1529. By its articles Pope Clement accepted the no longer debatable Spanish preponderance in Italy and in witness thereof agreed wholeheartedly to welcome Charles on his prospective early arrival in the peninsula and to officiate in person in his planned ceremonious coronation as emperor. In exchange for these concessions the pope received a full and overflowing measure of return benefits. Not only was he restored as ruler of the State of the Church but he secured the emperor's pledge to put him again, if necessary by force, in possession of rebellious Florence. A further stipulation named Alessandro as the future ruler of Florence and to seal the political with a family alliance this putative son of Lorenzo, but much more probably the son of the pope, was affianced to Margaret, an illegitimate daughter of the emperor.

It would be voicing no more than an obvious judgment to affirm that the treaty of Barcelona sounded the knell of the Florentine republic. At the time this heart-breaking sentence was rendered the republic had just passed its second birthday. Never throughout that period of anxious waiting had the citizens been in doubt that they would be faced with a mortal crisis the moment Clement had recovered sufficient power to go into action against them. For over a year following their revolt, owing to the pope's continued impotence there had been no occasion for alarm. Then, promptly following the catastrophe suffered by the French army under Lautrec a sharp tension gripped the population. For a city with so disturbed a civil past as that of Florence the population had thus far been almost miraculously united. Nor did they on the approach of danger become divided in their devotion to the re-established republican system. However, while not a single voice was raised in behalf of the return of the Medici, it was inevitable that a citizen group belonging chiefly to the older and more reflective generation should register alarm over the prospect of actual war and studiously ponder means for avoiding it. Remembering the kindly spirit manifested by Clement during his earlier direct government of the city, these sober-minded citizens felt encouraged to hope for an arrangement with him, whereby, in return for the acknowledgment of some sort of formal headship, he would give his consent to the continued existence of the popular government to which they were fervidly attached.

As soon as this opinion ventured into the open, it aroused the vehement opposition of chiefly the younger generation. To these fiery Hotspurs their elders were not only playing with treason but were reckoning with a papal frame of mind unsupported by as much as a shred of evidence. Utterly right in the latter, if not in the former respect, the young patriots demonstrated so furiously against their hesitant opponents that they drove them from the positions of control and took over the government. It is clear that they constituted no better than a minority group in the city, but, as has happened over and over again in similar crises, they developed so powerful an emotional drive that they swept the whole population off its feet with a force like that of a summer cloudburst.

It was owing, and solely owing, to the fanatic spirit of its youthful radicals that Florence undertook to face the combined challenge of pope and emperor, and, foredoomed though it was to failure, to take the heroic stand extolled by poets and singers through the ages and to go down to defeat with flying banners. Far from irresolutely waiting until Charles and Clement had reached their agreement, the eager Florentine democrats, anticipating the worst, busied themselves feverishly with preparations for the coming struggle. They enlarged the national militia and intensified its training; they hired mercenaries under an approved leader; and convinced that the campaign would take the form of a siege of their city, they made the strengthening of the fortifications their supreme concern. It was generally held throughout the peninsula that the admirable circumvallation of Florence dating back to the fourteenth century had made the city impregnable. But the improvement of artillery since that period had radically changed the picture and moved the government to submit the altered situation to the study of a committee of experts. When, in January, 1529, Michelangelo, the foremost living artist of Florentine birth, was appointed as head of the works, we need feel no surprise over his choice since, a genius of universal scope, Michelangelo was held to be as competent in engineering as he had already proved himself to be in sculpture, painting, and architecture.

The labors of Michelangelo over the Florentine fortifications constitute so interesting a chapter of the famous siege and so curious an episode in his personal career that it may not be overlooked. To begin with, it reveals the great artist as a typical Florentine, who, in spite of the unforgotten patronage of the Magnificent Lorenzo in his needy youth, remained an uncorrupted republican at heart. Consequently, when the skies darkened over the city of his love he came eagerly to its support and, on being called into active service in its behalf, elaborated a plan for the strengthening of its defenses, the still traceable remains of which arouse deserved admiration. They make clear his capital recognition that unless the hill of San Miniato towering over the city from the southern bank of the Arno be embraced within the system of defense the town would be subjected to the enemy's cannonade and would quickly fall. In this persuasion he extended the existing wall to include San Miniato and thereby succeeded in making Florence uncapturable by direct assault. Then, with the work well advanced, Michelangelo suddenly vanished. The fact may not be blinked nor can it be excused on the abused and threadbare ground of his artistic temperament. Somebody managed to reach the great man with a tale of personal danger and, constitutionally timid as repeatedly throughout his life he proved himself to be, he impulsively took to his heels. When, after some days, he had recovered his balance, he made a penitent return and was generously forgiven. But he was not re-appointed governor of the fortifications.

By the military clauses of the Barcelona settlement the emperor undertook to furnish the army that was to operate against Florence, while the pope was saddled with its cost. By the early autumn of 1529 the imperial regiments under the supreme command of the prince of Orange began to make their appearance around the city. His very first survey of the fortifications convinced the prince that he would not be able to take the city by storm. Regretfully he decided on the slower method of starvation. But this plan, too, presented difficulties, since he did not command a sufficient number of troops completely to envelop so large a city and to block its many approaches. With an understandable reluctance the Florentines had been obliged once again to fall back, in part at least, on the condottiere system and raised Malatesta Baglioni of Perugia to the post of supreme commander. His plan to defeat the starvation tactics of the prince of Orange was to keep open for the entrance of supplies to the densely populated city as many roads as possible, especially the westward roads connecting the city with the fertile region lying between it and the sea. The considerable success the plan achieved was exclusively due to a native Florentine, Francesco Ferrucci, who undertook to patrol the crucial area as a swift-moving partisan intent on keeping it clear of enemy invaders and on protecting the wagon trains that carried provisions to the city. Francesco was the first and the last soldier-hero Florence, so fertile in every other kind of talent that distinguishes our human kind, ever produced. His daring raids released a vast enthusiasm among the besieged population which, in spite of heavy losses, kept his ranks replenished with a steady flow of citizen volunteers.

However, when during the spring and summer of the following year Orange was strengthened by reinforcements dispatched to him from every point of the compass, Francesco Ferrucci found his field of operations progressively narrowed and a throttling noose drawn more and more tightly about his neck. Early in August he tried to break through a vastly superior environing host and was together with his faithful band smothered under the weight of enemy numbers. He had gone down in heroic combat but he had gone down. The starved population read their own fate in his but stubbornly refused to bend the knee to the victor. It was left to the foreign condottiere, Malatesta Baglioni, to take the no longer avoidable step of submission. Then and ever afterward the native historians have with all but complete unanimity pilloried him as the scum of his tribe, as the traitorous kin of Judas, but the judgment, at least in this uncompromising form, cannot stand up in the face of the evidence. True, when in June or July the scales had begun to be tipped against Florence, Baglioni had opened secret negotiations with the enemy. This was undoubtedly treason, in mitigation of which he might, not without a show of reason, have urged that Florence was tottering on its last legs and that the saving it from a fate like the recent frightful sack of Rome had become the legitimate concern of the commanding general.

Throughout the unusually severe winter of 1529-30 the condottiere had shared with the besieged the hope that the worst consequences of defeat might be avoided by the softening of the emperor's heart toward them. The faint glimmer was not finally extinguished until the reconciliation of pope and emperor, foreshadowed in their treaty of alliance, had been carried out to the last detail. True to the Barcelona time-table Charles had arrived at Genoa in the late summer of 1529 and had slowly made his way to Bologna, where he had set up his court. There, in the course of the following weeks, he signed the treaties with the many small states of Italy which confirmed his agreed peninsular supremacy. Humbly and repeatedly the beleaguered government of Florence besought him by special embassies not to consent to its destruction. His invariable answer was to refer the petitioners to his ally, the pope. In short, he stood unwaveringly by the treaty which had made him master of Italy subject to his concessions to the head of the Catholic church. What to his mind was the culminating feature of his alliance with Clement VII was fulfilled on February 24, 1530, at his temporary capital of Bologna. On that day and in that town, in a scene of unrivaled magnificence he received the imperial crown at the hands of his reconciled papal enemy.

In the circumstances help to Florence from Charles V could not be expected and was not forthcoming. However, we may not ignore the fact that when, on August 12, the Florentine signory, under the no longer concealed pressure of Malatesta Baglioni, signed the articles of surrender, it was expressly stated therein that the city had submitted not to the pope but to the emperor who, within a stipulated number of months, would determine its future government. The form given the treaty was intended to make the surrender appear somewhat less abject in the eyes of the conquered. But the concession to Florentine pride was not worth the ink spilled to record it. A week after the entrance of the victors into the city the citizens were summoned to a parlamentum conducted on the but too familiar fraudulent terms. With only Medicean partisans admitted to the piazza, they shouted their pre-arranged acceptance of a balia authorized to "reform" the government. The outcome of the "reform" was and could not be other than the re-establishment of the hated Medicean regime.

XIV

THE RULE OF ALESSANDRO, FIRST AND LAST
DUKE OF FLORENCE OF THE OLDER
MEDICEAN LINE

BRUSHING aside the ambiguous language, written and
spoken, employed in connection with the surrender of Florence, we are left in no doubt that the upshot of the defeat was
the restoration of Clement VII to the rule of the city. Since, as
obliged by his office, he continued to reside at Rome, he gov-
erned Florence through the Medicean balìa created by the August parlamentum. The fierce bias of these partisans was disclosed by the vengeful punishments of imprisonment, exile, and
death they dealt out to all the leaders of the fallen republic on
whom they succeeded in laying their hands. If the crushing of
their enemies would turn the trick, there was never again to
be a rising against the ruling house.

However, to proceed with too much precipitation accorded
neither with the cautious nature nor the political interest of
Clement. He could not be other than properly considerate of
an ally without whom he would never have been re-possessed

of Florence and to whom, moreover, and not to himself, the city had made formal submission. The treaty had even gone so far as to refer the future government of Florence to the emperor's sole decision. Undeniably, however, Clement had solid grounds for believing that the imperial verdict would, when issued, favor the Medicean cause. There, to begin with, was the Barcelona alliance with its string of solemn commitments to the pope. A perhaps even stronger reason for confidently banking on the continued attachment of Charles to his ally was the stipulation in their treaty by which the bastard Alessandro was named as the future ruler of Florence and, to buttress his feeble authority, had been affianced to Margaret, the emperor's illegitimate daughter.

The pope's confidence in the emperor's observation of the terms of their league was shown to be fully justified when, almost a year after the Florentines had put their fate in his hands, he delivered his sentence. By solemn charter under the imperial seal he declared that the government of the city should henceforth rest with Alessandro and his heirs after him with the proviso, however, that they were to exercise their power under the traditional, time-honored Florentine constitution. With the way thus smoothed for him, on July 5, 1531, the twenty-year-old Alessandro made his formal entrance into the city. While Clement at Rome had every reason to rejoice at the establishment of the young man as the head of the state with the invaluable blessing of the most powerful sovereign of Europe, still there was more than a drop of wormwood in his heady cup. The clause bringing back the old constitution was utterly repugnant to him, since it preserved a democratic germ by which the hope of freedom had been kept alive in the past and through which it might readily be again revived.

In April, 1532, with, we may be sure, the connivance of his faithful ally, Clement issued an order from Rome which abolished the old constitution and named Alessandro hereditary duke. Not to alarm the citizens with a too suddenly imposed unchecked absolutism the papal rescript created a number of appointive bodies with which the new duke was expected to take counsel. Pure window-dressing, they were before long completely ignored. The memorable historical fact is that with the naming of Alessandro as duke the pope had pronounced sentence of death upon the two-hundred-and-fifty-year-old republic of his native city. Although it cannot be denied that it had been in process of decline for some generations past and, more especially, from the time of the usurpation of Cosimo de' Medici, it had nonetheless never quite given up the ghost and on two recent occasions had with notable success renewed its youth. With the proclamation in 1532 of Florence as a duchy the republic was laid in its grave never to rise again. It was finished.

On first taking over the headship of the state Duke Alessandro gave close attention to his duties and, in spite of his unattractive personal appearance, won a measure of popular favor. He was a youth of robust health and, though boorish and uncultivated, not without a spark of native intelligence. He was held, against his will and inclination, to the moderate policy he followed by the beneficent restraint put on him by his papal sponsor at Rome. Regrettably this check was all too soon removed by the demise of Clement VII in 1534. Although only in his middle years, the pope had been failing in health for some time and his death did not come as a surprise. Almost uniformly unfortunate throughout his reign he had brought down on his bowed head a harsh and unqualified contempt, which later generations down to our own day have not seen fit to soften. In bidding this second pontiff of the house of Medici farewell it behooves our charity to recall that his rule befell among circumstances as difficult as any that have ever confronted a head of the church. Ground, politically, between the overpowering, competitive might of France and Spain, he was, in addition, faced with a rebellious secession from the church, for which he was not responsible and which he could not stay, of ever growing segments of northern Europe.

One act of Clement's, however, stands out from his wretched record and continues to excite our gratitude. It is to him that the world owes the New Sacristy of San Lorenzo with the amazing Medicean tombs, the greatest handiwork within the Florentine limits of its greatest sculptor. We noted on the occasion of the famous siege that Michelangelo was, like the average middle class Florentine, an anti-Medicean republican and that in 1529 he played an important role as head of the fortifications until, through a weakness of character that may not be glossed over, he took to flight. The most plausible explanation of his indefensible act is that, wholly absorbed in his artistic projects, he was not only unfamiliar with the machinations of politics but easily frightened by their uncomprehended manifestations to the point of panic. While this frame of mind defines him as a citizen in whom it was not safe to place too much reliance, it does not alter the fact that he was a committed republican. It is a permissible assumption that his republicanism dated from his birth and that, though it was softened somewhat by the bounty extended to him in his hard-pressed youth by Lorenzo the Magnificent, it was lodged deep in the marrow of his being.

In faithful acceptance of the Medicean tradition of patronage Pope Leo X had drawn Michelangelo into his service but had not employed him very wisely when he ordered him to provide the church of San Lorenzo with the façade, which through a long chain of mishaps it never received. On Leo's death, Clement VII, at that time still a cardinal, took over the rule of Florence and showed a much more intelligent appreciation of Michelangelo's genius. In close consultation with the artist he projected a new and more spacious sacristy to be added to the already extensive San Lorenzo compound. It was not planned as literally a sacristy but rather as a mausoleum to be filled with the bones and sculptured memorials of the more recent Medici dead.

The New Sacristy is a medium-sized, rectangular structure crowned by a dome. It is constructed in accordance with the classical principles re-introduced by Brunelleschi but employed by the flexible spirit of Michelangelo with a freedom and refinement that point to a later stage of development. Among the most recent Medici dead at the time of its construction were Giuliano, known as duke of Nemours, and Lorenzo, who by Leo X's base machinations had won the title of duke of Urbino. In the far-spreading genealogical tree of the family it would have been difficult to light upon two more insignificant representatives than these but, owing to the fact that they had recently died, they became eligible for marble memorials, the details of which Pope Clement with unusual and wholly praiseworthy humility left to the famous sculptor's exclusive discretion.

In the course of his uninterrupted artistic development Michelangelo had come to abandon the meticulous realism of his immediate Florentine predecessors, such as Donatello and Verrocchio, and to express himself less in fleeting individualist than in general idealist terms. As a result, instead of portrait statues of the two spurious dukes, he embodied under their respective names the two universal concepts of "action" and "reflection." One of the dukes, it does not in the least matter which one since in neither case was the actual personality taken into consideration, is represented as a soldier on the point of rising alertly from a seated position to issue a command, while the other duke, with chin dropped into his hand and his face shadowed by his helmet, is represented as brooding over problems which, vaster than war, plumb the depths of life itself.

The appeal inherent in the two figures stems from their reaching, like the Greek sculptures from which they unmistakably derive, beyond the narrow world of sense into the boundless world of thought; and this identical character is stamped on the allegorical figures which decorate the sarcophagi reposing at the feet of the two commemorated dead and holding their respective bodily remains. No one has ever been able to say with assurance what the allegories—a complementary male and female figure for each sarcophagus—signify, but no one attuned

to the mysteries which envelop our existence fails to be strangely
shaken by their unplumbed message. Michelangelo, when ques-
tioned as to their meaning, is said to have responded cryptically:
"Time which consumes all things." And that is as satisfying an
explanation as any that has ever been offered.

There was a corrupt core to Duke Alessandro which blossomed extravagantly on the death of his papal mentor who, as
we are aware, was in all probability also his father. He indulged
himself with less and less restraint in the sexual excesses to which
his nature violently inclined and progressively abandoned the
humane principles of government by which he seemed at first
to be guided. Before long he had completely made himself over
according to the vicious tyrant pattern of the age. He transformed his originally burgher household into a ducal court, went
about the streets with a clanking bodyguard, and sought security against a popular rising by a powerful fortress which, built
into the city wall, has survived to this day.

If no rising against Alessandro took place, the explanation
lies in part in the awful bloodletting of the recent siege, in even
larger part in the protection afforded the hated upstart by the
master of Italy, by Charles V. While, owing to the girl's youth,
the agreed union with the emperor's illegitimate daughter had
to be adjourned, Alessandro drew great, if imponderable,
strength from the mere fact of his being the emperor's prospective son-in-law. Not till February, 1536, by which time Margaret had passed her fourteenth birthday, did the long delayed
espousals take place. Less than a year later the bridegroom perished, not in a popular insurrection, which in the light of history
would seem to have been his fated end, but by the hand of an
assassin who acted on his own counsel and without the aid of a
single fellow-conspirator.

Since it was universally recognized that the sword and buckler
throughout the reign of the execrable tyrant was the emperor,
it is interesting to note that the only serious effort to supplant

him by citizen action took the form of a direct appeal for relief to Charles; and it is doubly interesting that the leader in this movement was Ippolito, that other Medici bastard, who by Pope Clement's original intention was to have been associated in the government of Florence with Alessandro. By the time the treaty of Barcelona of 1529 saw the light Clement had revised himself and by that document had named his ugly duckling, Alessandro, as the single and exclusive heir to the Arno city.

The disappointment of the handsome and highly endowed Ippolito over his rejection vented itself in violent scenes with the pope and was officially, but far from actually, overcome by the Holy Father's making such amends as he could by raising Ippolito to a cardinalate. So far was this distribution of favors to the latter's taste that there was henceforth open war between the two rival and envenomed cousins. Shortly after Clement's death Ippolito, who lived chiefly at Rome, entered into a conspiracy with representatives of leading Florentine families looking to the removal of the oppressor. The plan was to carry the case against Alessandro directly to the judgment bar of his all-powerful champion, Charles V. But as the young cardinal, the chosen spokesman of the conspiratorial group, was at the point of embarkation from a south-Italian port, he was laid low by the poisonous exhalations from the Pontine marshes above Naples and died after a few days.

With the demise of his most irreconcilable enemy in the summer of 1535 and the solemnization of his long adjourned marriage with the emperor's daughter in 1536, Duke Alessandro must have been thinking of himself as visibly favored by the gods when his fate caught up with him in the guise of the preferred associate of his pleasures, who was also his next of kin. This was Lorenzino de' Medici, who rid Florence of its ducal incubus by one of the most sensational murders in the revolting murder record of an age as savagely addicted to bloodshed and violence as any reported in human history.

✦

With Lorenzino we come upon the younger branch of the house of Medici which has thus far but rarely broken into our story. It was Lorenzo, the younger brother of Cosimo, founder of the older line, from whom the younger line stemmed. The close understanding which ruled the relations of the two branches for several decades was not even impaired by the difficulties usual to the distribution of a vast family estate among the heirs. It was not until the third generation that quarrels made their appearance which then mounted to an explosive climax with the expulsion from Florence in 1494 of the older line. From accumulated rancor against their relatives but also in the hope of saving their property from certain confiscation the two Medici who in that revolutionary year were the living representatives of the younger branch repudiated every connection with their ejected kin. They even went the length of shedding the Medici name and, in sign of their happily recovered republican origin, with a monumental lack of humor assumed the transparently fabricated name of Popolani. Although on the restoration of their relatives in 1512 they re-assumed their historical designation, they were rated as self-confessed renegades by Popes Leo X and Clement VII and obstinately refused recognition as bona fide members of the family.

By the time Alessandro became duke of Florence the two original Popolani had died and were represented among the living, the older Popolano by an eighteen-year-old youth named Lorenzo, the younger Popolano by a youth or rather boy of thirteen named Cosimo. Owing to his slender diminutive figure, Lorenzo was never referred to as other than Lorenzino, and since he had an insinuating way with him and Duke Alessandro had had no personal share in the cleavage between the two branches of the house, Lorenzino succeeded in flattering himself into a steadily expanding place in Alessandro's affection. In the course of Alessandro's five-year rule the association of the two young relatives grew visibly more intimate until they were taken by their countrymen to have become inseparable boon companions and Lorenzino shared with Alessandro the contempt originally visited on Alessandro alone. Such was the public assessment of the two Medici cronies when the city awakened on the morning of January 6, 1537, to be dumbfounded with the news that Lorenzino had murdered Alessandro in the night.

The possible motives of the assassination have been debated in scores of pamphlets and books in the intervening years without their authors having come to a common conclusion. The debate has turned in the main about the question as to whether the murder was an act of petty personal revenge or was prompted by the high, or at least high-sounding, political motives implied in the term tyrannicide and lauded to the skies in that age by a school of humanist writers who had taken over the concept from the ancient Greeks. Only in case it was tyrannicide has the murder any claim to historical consideration, and only in case the defense, in which Lorenzino presented his act in that light, is accepted at face value can the tyrannicide claim be sustained. Lorenzino's defense appeared under the name of *Apology* [1] and was composed in the city of Venice, to which he had fled immediately after committing his crime. While no generous spirit is capable of reading the *Apology,* which discloses itself as a straight outpouring of the heart, without being deeply moved, nonetheless so many unresolved considerations remain tied up with it that a cautious judge will hesitate to accept it as the full and unadulterated truth. Why, for instance, if Lorenzino was driven by an inner voice to deliver Florence from a vicious tyrant, did he not remain in the city and follow up his liberating act by leading a popular movement for the restoration of the republic? And is it possible to accept his explanation that he ran away with the plan of returning to lead the democratic forces as soon as they had organized the confidently expected rising?

[1] *The Apology* has been frequently printed. Among others by Roscoe, *Lorenzo de' Medici* (vol. II, Appendix).

If Lorenzino really believed that his act would sound the tocsin summoning the Florentines to a new outburst of republican heroism, he was as sharply disappointed as any disillusioned leader that had ever figured in their history. The people received the news of the murder of the tyrant with a benumbed astonishment and did not lift a finger to send the ducal regime after the duke. Their passivity enabled a resolute youth to come forward and establish himself in the seat of power before a successful protest could gather momentum. This was the not yet eighteen-year-old Cosimo, cousin of Lorenzino and leading available representative of the younger Medicean line. There was as yet no law of succession to which he could appeal in support of his claim. Nonetheless, something akin to a monarchy had recently taken shape in the person of Duke Alessandro and with some show of reason Cosimo could present himself as Alessandro's successor in the capacity of next of kin. In strict point of fact Lorenzino, as older than Cosimo, could on this same score have advanced a claim superior to that of Cosimo, but since one of Cosimo's earliest acts on seizing the scepter had been to outlaw the murderer and put a price on his head, he cunningly rid himself by that monarchical gesture of his most formidable rival. It deserves recording that the price on Lorenzino's head was not paid till eleven years later, when two members of the breed of professional murderers, who, called *bravi,* served the criminal purposes of that age, succeeded in stabbing Lorenzino to death as he issued with less than his usual caution from his Venetian hide-out.

In sharp distinction from the puny Lorenzino, Cosimo was a tall, powerfully built young man with a passionate love of sport of every kind, a better than average intelligence, and a rude drive for political power. As Duke Cosimo I he reigned for an exceedingly crucial term of years stretching from 1537 to 1574. In that period he so thoroughly reorganized the state that at his death it presented itself to view in the form and extent which it substantially retained until the momentous changes precipitated throughout Europe by the French Revolution. He, the second duke, and not Alessandro, the first duke, is the true founder of the Medicean monarchy. This clean-cut judgment, which cannot be successfully challenged, digs an unbridgeable gulf between the older and the younger branches of the house of Medici and justifies the contention that it is the older branch alone which is inseparably interwoven with the Florentine republic both in respect of its political vicissitudes and its cultural achievements.

With the accession to power of the younger Medicean line Florence underwent so fundamental a transformation that, except in physical appearance, it gave the impression of having become a different city. First and foremost among the striking changes was the absolute regime imposed by the new master. Only a blind partisan of the vanished republic would contend that this signified a total decline without a single redeeming feature. Duke Cosimo I conferred on the state converted into the duchy and, before long, into the grandduchy of Tuscany a public order and security the republic had never been able to bring about. While this may not be denied, it is clear that the administrative improvement was purchased at the cost of reducing the once high-spirited free citizens to groveling subjects receiving their laws from a sovereign, who, indifferent to their consent, owed his authority solely to military force. Let it also be conceded that the magnificent cultural impetus which the republic had sustained through several centuries continued to manifest itself sporadically throughout at least the first few decades of the absolutist regime. But its manifest enfeeblement, in spite of the continued lavish patronage of the princely heads of the state, afforded proof, if proof were needed, that the amazing Florentine culture, now slowly moving to extinction, was the product of the civil liberty which after a healthily contentious existence of three hundred years had been dealt its death-blow with the crushing of the heroic revolutionary upflare of

1530 by the combined action of the two greatest powers of Europe, the emperor and the pope.

Like every political form to which contriving man has given birth, the monarchy headed by Cosimo I and his successors has a history, but it is a history so dull and unrewarding that few people have ever been tempted to dip into it even superficially. Against that uninspiring record the history of the superseded Florentine republic stands out in sharpest conceivable contrast, since it reveals the restless political striving and incomparable cultural burgeoning of one of the most creative communities within the whole compass of Western civilization. And of that republican history the segment dominated by Cosimo de' Medici and his direct descendants and singled out for treatment in this book covers a hundred-year span which embraces that history's culminating as well as its declining and expiring phase.

THE HOUSE OF MEDICI

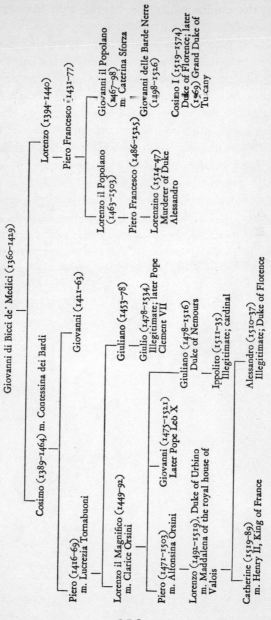

Giovanni di Bicci de' Medici (1360–1429)

Cosimo (1389–1464) m. Contessina dei Bardi

Lorenzo (1394–1440)

Piero Francesco (1431–77)

Giovanni il Popolano (1467–98) m. Caterina Sforza

Giovanni delle Barde Nerre (1498–1526)

Cosimo I (1519–1574) Duke of Florence; later (1569) Grand Duke of Tu-cany

Lorenzo il Popolano (1463–1503)

Piero Francesco (1486–1525)

Lorenzino (1514–47) Murderer of Duke Alessandro

Giovanni (1421–63)

Giuliano (1453–78)

Giulio (1478–1534) Illegitimate; later Pope Clement VII

Giuliano (1478–1516) Duke of Nemours

Ippolito (1511–35) Illegitimate; cardinal

Alessandro (1510–37) Illegitimate; Duke of Florence

Piero (1416–69) m. Lucrezia Tornabuoni

Lorenzo il Magnifico (1449–92) m. Clarice Orsini

Giovanni (1475–1521) Later Pope Leo X

Piero (1471–1503) m. Alfonsina Orsini

Lorenzo (1492–1519), Duke of Urbino m. Maddalena of the royal house of Valois

Catherine (1519–89) m. Henry II, King of France

225

BIBLIOGRAPHICAL NOTE

SINCE this book is not addressed to scholars, it was considered proper not to litter its pages with footnotes. While an exhaustive scholarly bibliography is equally inappropriate, a short selective reading list may not be unwelcome to the reader. It is here offered in two sections, the first carrying socio-political titles, the second works in the fields of Literature and the Fine Arts.

Cronica di Giovanni Villani. 4 vols. Florence, 1844-45.

Niccolò Machiavelli, *Istorie Fiorentine.* Numerous editions; also numerous English translations under the title *History of Florence.*

Benedetto Varchi, *Storia Fiorentina.* 3 vols. Florence, 1838-41.

Robert Davidsohn, *Geschichte von Florenz.* 4 vols. Berlin, 1896-1927. Indispensable for the medieval period.

F. T. Perrens, *Histoire de Florence.* 9 vols. Paris, 1877-1888.

G. A. Capponi, *Storia della Repubblica di Firenze.* 2 vols. Florence, 1875.

Ferdinand Schevill, *History of Florence.* Harcourt, Brace and Co., 1936. An Introduction reviews the sources of Florentine history under the title "On Florentine Historiography."

F. A. Hyett, *Florence: Her History and Art to the Fall of the Republic.* London, 1903.

G. F. Young, *The Medici*. The Modern Library. The subjective divagations of a sentimentalist with a mind above history.

G. Pieraccini, *La Stirpe dei Medici di Cafaggiolo*. 3 vols. Florence, 1925.

C. S. Gutkind, *Cosimo de' Medici*. New York, 1938.

William Roscoe, *The Life of Lorenzo de' Medici*. Published 1797. With numerous editions since.

William Roscoe, *The Life of Leo X*. Many editions.

Edward Armstrong, *Lorenzo de' Medici*. London, 1896.

E. L. S. Horsburgh, *Lorenzo the Magnificent and Florence in Her Golden Age*. London, 1909.

E. Barfucci, *Lorenzo de' Medici*. Florence, 1945. With a wealth of illustrations bearing on Lorenzo and his times.

Raymond de Roover, *The Medici Bank*. Journal of Economic History, VI, no. 1 (1946).

F. E. de Roover, *Francesco Sassetti and the Downfall of the Medici Banking House*. Bulletin of the Business Historical Society, XVII (1943).

Giorgio Vasari, *Le Vite de' più eccellenti pittori, scultori, ed architetti*. Ed. by G. Milanesi. 9 vols. Florence, 1906. Of the many English translations I name that of A. B. Hinds. 4 vols., 1927.

Adolfo Venturi, *A Short History of Italian Art*. Macmillan, 1926.

J. C. Burckhardt, *The Civilization of the Renaissance in Italy*. Harper, 1929.

John A. Symonds, *The Revival of Learning*, *The Fine Arts* volumes of his *Renaissance in Italy*. 7 vols., Holt, 1888.

W. J. Anderson, *The Architecture of the Renaissance in Italy*. Scribner, 1927.

Wilhelm von Bode, *Florentine Sculptors of the Renaissance*. Scribner, 1909.

F. J. Mather, Jr., *A History of Italian Painting*. Holt, 1923.

Heinrich Wölfflin, *The Art of the Italian Renaissance*. Putnam, 1913.

Bernhard Berenson, *The Florentine Painters of the Renaissance*. Putnam, 1909.

Richard Offner, *Italian Primitives at Yale University*. Yale University Press, 1927.

INDEX

Accoppiatori, electoral device of Cosimo, 70; abolished and restored, 81-83

Albizzi, Maso degli, oligarchic rule by, 37-38, 57-58

Albizzi, Rinaldo degli, son of Maso, leading oligarch, 38; directs attack on Lucca, 38-39; supports the catasto, 59; loses war with Lucca, 59-60; origin of conflict with Cosimo de' Medici, 60-62; defeat and banishment of, 64-65; vainly attacks Florence (1440), 75-76

Alexander III, pope, triumphs over Frederick I, 11

Alexander VI, pope, chief agent in destruction of Savonarola, 175

Altopascio, battle of (1325), 27

Alum, use of described, 120; deposit found near Volterra, 121

Angelico, Fra, his work described, 99-100

Anghiari, battle of (1440), 76

Anjou, count of, afterwards King Charles of Sicily, 15

Anjou, house of, established in Sicily, 15; retains claim to Naples, 138; dies out leaving claim to Naples to king of France, 138

Aragon, house of, acquires Sicily and Naples, 138

Architecture, medieval, in Florence, 48-51; Renaissance, stimulated by Brunelleschi, 51, 91; example of furnished by sacristy of San Lorenzo, 91

Arezzo, Florence makes war on, 22; Florence conquers, 36

Arti. See Guilds

Badia, of Fiesole, erected by Cosimo, 88, 92

Badia, La, of Florence, bell-tower of, 49

Baglioni, Malatesta, condottiere, in charge of defense of Florence during siege, 210, 211

Balìa, device for a manipulated reform, 62, 70, 82-83, 111, 146, 183, 212

Bandini, Bernardo, his share in Pazzi conspiracy, 127; his capture and execution, 130

Baptistry. *See* San Giovanni

Barcelona, Treaty of (1529), 206

Bardi, family and trading company, 30; Cosimo marries Contessina dei Bardi, 105

Bargello (palace of the podestà), 50

Beneventum, battle of, 15

Birth of Venus, by Botticelli, 158

Index

Index

Nencia da Barberino, poem by Lorenzo, 161

Neoplatonism, described, 156-159, 164-165

Neroni, Diotisalvi, rebels against rule of Medici, 81, 109, 111

Niccolò da Uzzano, member of Albizzi oligarchy, 38; supports the catasto of 1428, 59

Niccolò Niccoli, book collector, 87; his books given to San Marco library by Cosimo, 87

Oligarchy, rules at Florence, 6, 20; unsuccessfully challenged by democracy, 31-34

Orange, prince of, commands emperor's army at siege of Florence, 209, 210

Or San Michele, a Gothic structure, 49

Orcagna, fashions tabernacle of Or San Michele, 49, 52

Ordinances of Justice, described, 19-20

Orléans, duke of, claims Milan through his Visconti descent, 138

Orsini, Alfonsina, wife of Piero de' Medici, 147

Orsini, Clarice, marries Lorenzo (1469), 115; mother of six children, 146; death of (1488), 146

Otranto, captured by the Turks (1480) and regained by Naples, 133

Palazzo Vecchio (Palace of the Priors), leading civic structure, 50

Paleologus, John, Greek emperor comes to Florence (1439), 74

Palle, Medicean coat of arms, 113; embellished with three French lilies (1465), 113

Papacy, relation to empire by medieval theory, 10-11; victory over Henry IV, 11; victory over Frederick I, 11; in alliance with communes against emperor, 11-13

Parlamentum, origin of, 7; abuse of by Albizzi and Medici, 61-62; mocking use of, 82-83, 111, 146, 183-184, 212

Passerini, Cardinal, 203, 204

Pater Patriae, title accorded Cosimo, 105

Pavia, battle of (1525), 199

Pazzi, Florentine magnate family, develops rival bank to Medici, 125; pardoned by Lorenzo, 167

Pazzi, Francesco, his share in plot against the Medici, 125-127; 167

Pazzi, Guglielmo, married to Bianca, daughter of Lorenzo, 167

Pazzi, Jacopo, his share in the Pazzi plot (1478), 127-129; 167

Pazzi Plot (The), origin and development of, 125-130

Peruzzi, early trading company, 30

Petrarch, Francesco, poet and humanist, 44-45

Piccinino, general of Duke Filippo Maria of Milan, 75

Pico della Mirandola, 149; his labors as Platonist, 156-157

Pisa, leading commune of Tuscany, 5, 6: conflict with Florence, 22, 23; wins headship of Tuscany under Uguccione della Faggiuola, 25-26; conquered by Florence (1406), 36; university established by Lorenzo at, 154-155

Pisano, Andrea, sculptor of the first baptistry gate, 52

Pisano, Giovanni, leading Gothic sculptor, 52

Pistoia, captured by Lucca, 26